Andrew DeCort

BLESSED ARE THE OTHERS

Jesus' Way in a Violent World

For Padre, my dear old dad
Joe DeCort Jr. (1944-2024)
"It hurts so good"

Published by

 BitterSweetBooks

ISBN 978-1-958865-06-4

Editing by Kate Schmidgall, Peter Hartwig, and Avery Marks
Cover art by Obiekwe Okolo derived from Pillars of Creation (NIRCam Image) by NASA, ESA, CSA, STScI; Joseph DePasquale (STScI), Anton M. Koekemoer (STScI), Alyssa Pagan (STScI).

Typesetting by Greg Sitzmann
Production and operations by Dave Baker

Praise for *Blessed Are the Others*

"This book is required reading for those who understand the need for a deep connection between subtle analysis and empowered spirituality, especially as it relates to the prophetic Christian tradition!"

Dr. Cornel West, Dietrich Bonhoeffer Professor of Philosophy & Christian Practice at Union Theological Seminary, author of *Race Matters*

"*Blessed Are the Others* is a profound and transformative journey into the depths of human suffering, resilience, and the pursuit of justice. Through personal narratives, historical reflections, and spiritual wisdom, Andrew DeCort challenges understandings of compassion, equips us to navigate complexity with grace and courage, and invites us into the paradoxical joys of Jesus' 'Beatitudinal Way.'"

Dr. Noah Toly, Provost of Calvin University

"In this powerful new book, Andrew DeCort shows us that ancient sacred texts can still serve as anchors and guides for how to live and treat one another in the modern world."

Dr. Eboo Patel, Founder and President of Interfaith America

"Andrew DeCort pushes the proverbial envelope with this book. He leans into the sacred text of Scripture as a means of navigating this cultural moment with compassion and conviction. It will challenge your thinking and living."

Mark Batterson, *New York Times* bestselling author of *The Circle Maker*

"Andrew DeCort has a rare ability to articulate the power of Christian faith in ways which are compelling and persuasive for even the most avowedly atheistic minds. This raw, brutally honest new book is an inspiration."

Tom Gardner, Africa Correspondent, *The Economist*

"When Andrew showed up in Ethiopia, he could have been treated like a king. Instead, he chose to stand as a peacemaker with the outcasts of our society, the victims of violence and ridicule. And so, he became the other and was treated like a leper, prostitute, and tax collector. This is a memoir most Ethiopians will relate to, a moving testament of life filled with grief, hope, and joy."

Dr. Abadir Ibrahim, Associate Director of The Human Rights Program, Harvard Law School

"Who could we become if we dare to get out of our own way and lean into the path of the holy? In *Blessed Are the Others*, Andrew journeys with us as we follow the light toward the answer. This work is such a gorgeous gift. It is a balm for today and bread for tomorrow."

Candice Benbow, author of *Red Lip Theology*

"This is a fearsome book—in the best of ways. Sometimes I fear too many of us have made Jesus into a stop sign, when he actually came to be a doorway. Andrew DeCort pierces through the abstraction of salvation by dint of his own long-suffering, searching, and a rare, tenacious hope. This is a book for all those looking for a Way that can be lived—here, now, and not alone."

Anne Snyder, Editor-in-chief of *Comment*

"Despite some disagreements, I applaud this fine reflection on the Beatitudes for its intense vividness, its bracing personal honesty, its profound sourcing in people like Etty Hillesum and James Baldwin, its emergence from a place of acute pain, and thus its ability to identify with Jesus' own pain and the pain of so many others."

Rev. Dr. David Gushee, Past President of The American Academy of Religion and The Society of Christian Ethics

"In a time marked by division, anger, fracture, and contempt, Andrew DeCort's luminous work *Blessed Are the Others* explores a way of living in the world and loving its inhabitants that is both countercultural and ancient: the Beatitudinal Way. DeCort uncovers what it means to be blessed in Jesus' Sermon on the Mount, and illuminates the invitation to 'humane happiness' and radical compassion that Jesus extends. It is a work that will both challenge and bless."

Cherie Harder, President of The Trinity Forum

"I thoroughly love this book. I love its simplicity, elegance, and truthful honesty. Andrew invites us to learn to embrace our poverty, grief, and brokenness. Only in that embrace can we become blessed, peacemakers, true children of God. I'm grateful to Andrew for the gift of this book—and for sharing his own life's stories. We need more writers like Andrew who remind us of the true meaning of the Gospel."

Fr. Emmanuel Katongole, Catholic priest, Professor of Theology and Peace Studies at the University of Notre Dame

"This book is now stuck in my consciousness and will badger me for years to come. I'm irritated by it and do not want to endorse it. I have issues with DeCort's relationship with textual inspiration. As a Jewish reader, I take umbrage at his treatment of Moses. I do not find the 'Beatitudinal Way' to be something I'm excited to engage. But this book has changed me, despite all my misgivings. I am unsettled and will be working through this with my spiritual director. I imagine that is what it was like to listen to these teachings when Christ first gave them. My gratitude demands an endorsement and recommendation."

Marty Solomon, creator of *The BEMA Podcast*, author of *Asking Better Questions of the Bible*

"If anything is going to heal our broken world, it is going to be the truthful witness of the blessed ones. Those who are brave enough to take Christ's words at face value. The ones who cling to nothing but Christ, boast in nothing but Christ, and point us toward the hope found in the kingdom of God. This book is one such witness—tender, poetic, and stirring."

Jon Guerra, Devotional Music Singer-Songwriter

"This much-needed book provides a post-evangelical framework for elevating the life, teachings, and ministry of Jesus as an invitation to experience the kingdom of heaven here and now. Illuminating, inciting and inviting."

Keri Ladouceur, Executive Director of The Post-Evangelical Collective

"*Blessed Are the Others* takes us to the heart of the teachings of Jesus—the Sermon on the Mount—and challenges the reader to embrace the radical vulnerability and healing compassion of Jesus' core teaching. Andrew's book unpacks the powerful relevance of Jesus' words still today and the path of peace for our world, whether in the US or Palestine."

Dr. Munther Isaac, Academic Dean of Bethlehem Bible College in Palestine, Director of Christ at the Checkpoint Conference, Pastor of Christmas Evangelical Lutheran Church in Bethlehem

"Familiarity can lead us to miss what lies before us. Andrew DeCort invites us to engage the Beatitudes anew and to contend with our own ways of navigating our experiences of poverty in spirit. Take a walk with DeCort through horror, betrayal, and so much more. Dialogue with his views and squarely face your approach to life in an upside down world. You will find yourself considering again and again the truth about yourself and the challenging path of discipleship. Those who read this book with integrity will see why it is important to face the crucial questions of life over and over again. DeCort's life experience is as real as it gets."

Vincent Bacote, Professor of Theology, Director of the Center for Applied Christian Ethics, Wheaton College

"Andrew DeCort's *Blessed Are the Others* sketches the conversation between friends whose hearts are burning after hearing Jesus teach the Beatitudes, a divine justice manifesto calling for right relationships of mutual flourishing. DeCort's book explores the Beatitudinal Way as 'an endlessly generative, culturally divergent path of humane happiness.' DeCort layers the Beatitudinal Way like tree rings that embody the heart of

God within us, promising that as we integrate total belonging, we will stand and bear witness while honoring joy in the midst of the crimes of our times."

Marianne Abel-Lipschutz, Writer, Farmer, Advocate

"I devoured this book! I've taken two pilgrimages in the last several years to try and figure out how to become human again in the face of accelerating forms of empire, hopelessness, and despair. This book took me on another pilgrimage, another Camino, to dig into the question of how we become human, again, in the face of so much violence. I am in desperate need of relearning the Way, and digging into the Beatitudinal Way not only captures my imagination but holds my attention and compels me back into the teachings of Jesus. This book nurtures my own honest search for what is True, Good, and Beautiful, and I'm hopeful that at the end of empire, this book will prove a Way for us to suture ourselves and help us heal our wounds and commit to a life of peace and justice—the entangled roots of the teachings of Jesus."

Rev. Dr. Roberto Che Espinoza, Pastor of Union University Church, Visiting Professor at Duke Divinity School, Founder of Our Collective Becoming

"This is a brilliant, beautiful, and revolutionary book. Forged in the deepest pain, fear, and even despair, it spoke to mine. Short but never cheap, drawing on a vast depth of experience, knowledge, and mentors, Andrew DeCort's profound exploration of what a first century Middle Eastern carpenter has to say about the good life is, quite honestly, one of the best spirituality books I've read in years. This book opens the door not only to the what of Jesus' teaching but the why, and how even those scarred by religion with the very best reasons to reject it might find a home for those scars, and a way to be humanely happy, even amidst the worst of circumstances. It has been said that justice is what love looks like in public; *Blessed Are the Others* is what happens when personal truth meets that love, and gives itself to the rest of us. I'll be urging many people to read this book, and I'm so grateful it exists."

Gareth Higgins, Writer, Peacemaker, Co-Founder of The Porch Community

"Are you happy in this modern world?
Or do you need more?
Is there something else
you're searching for?
I'm falling.
In all the good times,
I find myself longing
for change.
And in the bad times,
I fear myself...
We're far from the shallow now."
Lady Gaga[1]

***

"The revolution which was begun two thousand years ago by a disreputable Hebrew criminal may now have to be begun again by people equally disreputable and equally improbable."
James Baldwin[2]

***

"Blessing means laying one's hand on something and saying: Despite everything, you belong to God. This is what we do with the world that inflicts such suffering on us."
Dietrich Bonhoeffer[3]

---

1 Lady Gaga, "Shallow," lead single to the soundtrack *A Star Is Born* (Interscope, 2018).

2 James Baldwin, "The Fire Next Time" in *James Baldwin: Collected Essays*, ed. Toni Morrison (New York, NY: Library of America, 1998), 312.

3 Dietrich Bonhoeffer, "Daily Text Meditation for June 7 and 8, 1944," in *Conspiracy and Imprisonment: 1940-1945: Dietrich Bonhoeffer Works*, Vol. 16, ed. Mark Brocker (Minneapolis, MN: Fortress Press, 2006), 632 (translation modified).

Table of Contents

Chapter 1 A Letter from Me to You   1

Chapter 2 The Trailhead to the Way   12

Chapter 3 Way-Station 1: Poverty   30
Crisis 1: Hardness or Grief?

Chapter 4 Way-Station 2: Grief   44
Crisis 2: Vengeance or Nonviolence?

Chapter 5 Way-Station 3: Nonviolence   58
Crisis 3: Withdrawal or Justice?

Chapter 6 Way-Station 4: Justice   75
Crisis 4: Condemnation or Compassion?

Chapter 7 Way-Station 5: Compassion   90
Crisis 5: Cynicism or Cleansing?

Chapter 8 Way-Station 6: Cleanheartedness   105
Crisis 6: Religion or Peacemaking?

Chapter 9 Way-Station 7: Peacemaking   122
Crisis 7: Approval or Persecution?

Chapter 10 Way-Station 8: Persecution   138

Chapter 11 Onward: The Beatitudinal Way   156

Appendices   162

Questions for Reflection   170

CHAPTER 1

A Letter From Me to You

*For Kate: Thank you
for birthing this book.*

"I come to you, defenses down,
with the trust of a child."[1]
Peter Gabriel

---

1 Peter Gabriel, "Red Rain," track 1 on *So* (Virgin Records, 1987).

Dear _____ (kindly insert your name),

I'm honored to address you.

This little book took me by surprise. I wasn't planning to write it. Honestly, I wasn't sure I could write at all anymore.

To get started, let me tell you a chapter of my story and how this book was born.

In November 2020, Ethiopia descended into a devastating civil war. As I write, it remains the deadliest conflict in the twenty-first century. An estimated 1.2 million people have been killed.

My work in Ethiopia focused on advocating for peace in grassroots communities and among senior religious, social, and political leaders. As Covid and calls for violence burst onto the national scene, a story started circulating that I was working to destroy the Ethiopian government.

This is when the death threats started.

My wife Lily and I were living in Addis Ababa on a major road near a big bridge in a neighborhood lined with butcher shops. All sorts of people, mainly Christians, started promising that they would kill me. They said they'd run me over with their cars, throw me off a bridge, or dismember my body. I received over fifty pages of this psychological terrorism.

These threats hit very close to home. They taught me an obvious but unpleasant lesson: peace is threatening when conflict is popular and profitable. Said differently, when you love "the enemy," you *become* the enemy.

This continued for three years. I was intensely committed to my work in Ethiopia and tried to press on. Lily and I sheltered in a safe house, limited our movements, and started wearing a tracking device in case we were kidnapped. But by May 2021, it became clear that it was time for us to transition.

"Exile" came with a poignancy I never anticipated knowing personally. More importantly and painfully, my work had cost Lily her home and the ability to be near her family. It's difficult to describe how soul-sickening it is to choose between (a) keeping quiet while millions of families are losing everything or (b) endangering your own family while achieving maybe nothing.

Eighteen months into leaving Ethiopia, now safe and seemingly sound, 2023 was perhaps the hardest year of my life.

In January, a fear started gnawing inside me that I would be abandoned by people I love. I found myself on my knees late at night with my face pressed into the carpet beside our bed. The hate messages had chipped away at my heart. I learned another painful lesson: hate is soul vandalism.

In the middle of January, a close friend stepped back from our relationship after we disagreed about the reach of God's love for his gay sister. He was a significant donor to our work, and our budget immediately became more precarious. I feared this was only the tip of an iceberg, the first domino in a chain reaction of loss.

In February, a viral media personality in Ethiopia—believed to be employed by the Prime Minister himself—began trashing my character on his TV show. Tens of thousands of people watched as this man strung together a conspiracy in which I was the mastermind behind a secret plot to destroy Ethiopia and dismantle her ancient church. He insisted that I had organized a major assassination that set off atrocious violence in Ethiopia. This dear brother raged with garrulous certainty.

More death threats followed.

Then in March, a large church in Chicago invited me to

speak at their annual leadership conference. They bought boxes of my new book *Flourishing on the Edge of Faith* and promised to give a copy to each of their staff members. This was welcome encouragement in a year off to a rough start. I was delighted.

But an influential Ethiopian pastor warned them that I was a dangerous teacher. I had recently given a talk at the United Arab Emirates Embassy in Ethiopia and suggested that God's invitation to love echoes across our diverse spiritual traditions—not just in Christianity. I called this "a sacred voice that can heal othering in a time of war."

The church took the pastor's word for it and disinvited me. My books were promptly returned, unread, to my publisher.

Now at the end of March, I was helping some dear friends move. It was a joyous occasion. Thom had gotten sober after years of alcoholism. Ellie had recently given birth to their adorable baby girl Ramona. She played on the floor as we shuffled furniture.

But in between loads, an alert popped up on my phone. I quickly learned that my identity had been stolen. Just like that, Lily and I were left with a mountain of debt and a wrecked credit score. Money had always been tight for us, but now our anxiety escalated. We crunched numbers and squinted to envision a viable financial future for ourselves.

Identify theft felt absurdly on the nose. I was struggling to prove the most basic facts about my birth, my work, my faith, and now my bank account.

Soon after, BitterSweet sent me with the Telos Group to Louisiana, Alabama, and Mississippi. My task was to write a story about Telos' inspiring peacemaking work in the heart of conflict zones, stretching from Israel/Palestine to America's Deep South. This powerful pilgrimage immersed me in America's history of slavery, segregation, mass incarceration, and ongoing racial injustice. I came away with over a hundred pages of typed notes.

But as I began writing the story in April, I found that I

simply couldn't *write*. I was tremendously inspired by the pilgrimage. Our private seminar with Reena Evers-Everette, daughter of the assassinated civil rights activist Medgar Evers, was especially moving.

Still, after years of advocating for peace in Ethiopia and being overwhelmed with grief in the face of violence, writing about more injustice felt like a screwdriver churning into the face of my soul. I was one small twist away from being stripped to my core and permanently mutilated.

Later in April, I found myself laying facedown on my friend Steve's wood floor, weeping uncontrollably. I couldn't bear to spend another moment concentrating on the cruelty we humans inflict on one another—trying to find words for the inexpressible. I despise breaking promises, but I had to abandon writing the story. Thankfully, my publisher was gracious.

Then on May 12, my family attended a local performance of *Fiddler on the Roof*. It was delightful. *Tradition!* But at the end of the show, I saw my sister Elizabeth weeping in the back with her face pressed against my dad's chest. That's when padre, as I call him, told me that he had cancer.

The thought flashed through my mind like lightning: "Is this what my gnawing fear of losing loved ones was *really* about? Is dad dying?" I soon became intimately familiar with the local oncology unit.

Throughout this seemingly endless winter, I felt incredibly empty inside.

I was working on a book that I had planned to write for several years. It was my spiritual manifesto. But like the BitterSweet story, the words simply wouldn't come out of me. I was dogged with self-doubt. My body tingled with anxious energy. I was aching inside but also strangely sterile.

This was maddening. Here I was, in a safe place, with

time to write—both of which felt like guilty luxuries in light of my Ethiopian family and friends' suffering. But I'd sit at my desk, and nothing would happen. Tears burst from my eyes in the presence of my friends. But I felt woefully inadequate, incapable, limp—like I was withering and had nothing to say, nothing to give, nothing but a cringe clinging to my soul. Perhaps nothing left to live for.

On a walk in the prairie, a bridge over a beautiful river tempted me with an easy escape. I ended up weeping for three hours on my little Camino.

Around this time, I started to fear that something was wrong with my brain, that I was losing my memory. My mind felt muddy, and I struggled to recall words—*pistachio*—and my friends' names. Was this Long Covid or early onset Alzheimer's? I read articles in medical journals late at night. Eventually, I reached out to the Covid Lab at my alma mater, the University of Chicago. But I didn't have health insurance and they refused to see me.

over

Ethiopia was whelmed with deth and distruction.

We were transitioning exiled and still under

Fear of rejection + abandonment festered.   attack.

Our finances were ruined.

Dad hAd CANCER.   IsOlation & depPrEssIon were SWALLOWING us.

Lily told me that she was in "*a constant state of **disappointment**.*"

It felt like my deepest loves—the things I had risked my life for—were withering away. I feared that this was me now, my new normal, an unhappy Andrew I desperately didn't want to be. The haunting question came back: *Is life worth living?*

On May 28, I celebrated my fortieth birthday in Maine with Lily and our dear friends Kate and David. It was a strange day of many mixed emotions. I was grateful to be alive, and David rebaptized me in the icy Atlantic Ocean. I wanted to do this sacred ritual again as an act of recommitting myself to the way of Jesus in the second half of my life. But my life was nothing like I had expected it to be even a few years before.

I felt like a failed adult.

**

Fast-forward to November 2023.

The leaves of Chicago's trees were beginning to flare and fall. Breathtaking paintings were on display in all directions. They swayed like dazzling afros everywhere you looked, fluttering through the air and dancing along the ground.

But autumn's magic beauty felt ominous to me. It signaled the onset of another brutal winter. More unsettling, it signaled the continuation of this longer, darker season weathering inside of me.

At the time I was scheduled to drive seven hundred miles across the country into the Shenandoah Mountains. My destination was the BitterSweet Annual Retreat. Kate, my publisher, had generously asked me to give a "grounding reflection" for the community.

But as the air became crisp and the sun fell over fallow fields, I felt like I still had *nothing*—such a total, definite word. Hamas had unleashed its murderous terror on October 7. Israel was devastating Gaza. A six-year-old Palestinian boy named Wadea had been brutally stabbed to death by a Christian nationalist ten miles from where I live.

The screwdriver was churning deeper. The soul vandalism was becoming acute.

BitterSweet gathers a small but mighty community of writers, editors, filmmakers, photographers, producers, and other artists and executives. They come together to tell stories that reject cynicism, defy apathy, and celebrate good. The organizations they cover offer an alternative orientation of hope to the addictive despair narrative in mainstream media. Kate once described BitterSweet's work as "the Beatitudinal Way."

I love and respect these people from the marrow of my bones. And this retreat was marking special milestones. BitterSweet was celebrating its hundredth story. It was also the first anniversary of my book *Flourishing on the Edge of Faith*.

But I wasn't flourishing. I felt intimidated to be among my friends, certain to disappoint them.

The BitterSweet community is suffused with a rare quality of loving presence. Its ecosystem is cooperative rather than competitive. Still, everyone there embodies exceptional motivation and accomplishment. Contemplating this, the cringe inside of me clenched tighter: *How did I publish a book with these people? How did I deceive* them *into thinking I was one of* them? (Have I mentioned my suffocating self-doubt?)

I planned to (im)politely cancel.

But Kate—endlessly kind and undaunted—got me on a plane to D.C. Soon enough, I was sitting on her hallowed porch, where I'm sitting again now. Her husband David, my rebaptizer, sat with me late into the night and asked me what I needed in this dark time of my life.

I knew the truth. But I didn't want to say it.
I needed to *cry*.

A discerning listener, David gently probed deeper. I confessed that I simply couldn't see the way forward for Lily's and my future. My vision was blocked, shrouded in fog. I felt stripped and blinded, confused and frightened. "I'm afraid our story is broken," I told him.

That's when I began to cry.

Something happened here that took me by total surprise. I'll return to it in chapter six.

The next morning, we packed up and drove into the Shenandoah Mountains. On the road, we passed billboards with polarizing political messages and massive American flags. Signs of our times.

A few hours later, we arrived at the Bellfry, Rev. Anne Grizzle's exceptionally thoughtful home and retreat center. As I stepped across the threshold, I looked down and saw etched into stone "He makes beauty from ashes." I knew I needed *that* to happen. But I wasn't sure it was possible, for me at least.

As the weekend unfolded, I slipped away as much as I could—up the narrow ladder into the solitary prayer tower with wide windows overlooking the mountains. I needed time to pray and prepare for my talk. But more honestly, I was hiding. I texted Lily that anxiety was escalating in me.

I spent a lot of time up there alone in silence. I listened to the rain tap on the roof. I watched the birds soar as the mist cleared over the mountains. I traveled in my mind to important memories with loved ones across the earth.

And finally, I felt like I'd been given something to share. It flowed out of me like water. It spoke to me, at least—to where I was in the bewildering, twenty-first-century polarization, poverty, and pain of my life.

But was there anything there for anyone else? Would my message disappoint Kate and my friends? Would it be boring? Too heavy? So obvious and oversimple as to be unworthy of their precious time and attention?

***

The next morning, Kate invited me to sit at the hearth of the fireplace and share my "grounding reflection" with our BitterSweet community.

Throughout the message, my friend Brandon, an internationally renowned filmmaker, wept. At the end, Obi, BitterSweet's creative director and the largest man in the room—both in personality and physical stature—tried to speak but broke down in tears. Afterward, Sameel, who serves as a senior executive for a global media company, came up to me, put his face on my shoulder without a word, and began to cry, like my sister Elizabeth did with padre.

It seems that many of us needed to cry. Other friends approached me in the hallway and asked, "Was that the skeleton for the book you're writing?"

It wasn't.

As I've mentioned, the book I was "writing" was woefully stuck in the slum of my soul's self-doubting emptiness. I felt like a fraud even saying that I was "writing" a book.

But then our host, Anne, asked me if this was the content for my next book. Like the others, I told her no. But Anne was more insistent. What she said moved me so deeply that I wrote it down:

> "This message is for such a time as this. Violence begets violence; then generations of violated become the violators; then more trauma. The whole thing is there: here is the Beatitudinal Way. We need it—for such a time as this. What you shared wasn't a rough draft but a beautiful symphony. That symphony is given, and when you're a prophet, you just have to speak what is given. Some things require a long pregnancy, and others just come."

Anne got at least one thing right: this book *just came*. At a time when I feared I was finished, something was being born inside of me. I was in a long labor without even realizing it, until *it* "just came."

I make no claim to be a prophet. I doubt people who do. But Anne, Kate and David, Bailey and my BitterSweet community encouraged me to share this unexpected book with a wider audience. They have my sincere thanks.

What you're holding is the fruit of their encouragement. Maybe even beauty from ashes. It's dedicated to my beloved dad, who died forty days ago.

I offer this book to you in hopes that it might encourage you in your journey of becoming human and finding true happiness. For short, I call this *humane happiness*. It's a primal kind of happiness that's deeply rooted in compassion and intertwined with the happiness of others.

Perhaps like me, you're also in labor. Maybe you're aching with poverty. Or groaning with grief. Or questioning if angry aggression or numbed withdrawl is your only way out. Maybe you're asking if life is worth living. I suspect we all share this vulnerable place, though we often suppress it.

Here Jesus of Nazareth invites us into a strange wisdom as ancient as the pillars of creation. He promises that opening ourselves to our pain is the beginning of the Beatitudinal Way. Paradoxically, this is the path of humane happiness.

Thank you for sharing your time and attention with my words so far from the shallow. We are not alone. We are not insane. We are human.

Yours with affection and gratitude,
Andrew

CHAPTER 2

The Trailhead
to the Way

For James Baldwin: Thank you
for your honesty.

"The great problem is how to be—in the best sense
of that kaleidoscopic word—a human."[1]
James Baldwin

---

1 James Baldwin, "The Fire Next Time" in *James Baldwin: Collected Essays*, ed. Toni Morrison
(New York, NY: Library of America, 1998), 232.

In this trailhead to our journey, I want to map out some of the terrain we'll travel together. We'll explore what "blessing" means, why Jesus is a worthy guide, and how we can navigate his eightfold path with its brilliant twists and our cultural pitfalls.

Like so many epic quests, I begin with a simple question: What is the Beatitudinal Way of Jesus?

The word "Beatitudinal" sounds a bit odd, I admit. But "beatitude" comes from the Latin word *beatus*. And *beatus* simply means "blessed." Today we call this flourishing, wellbeing, the good life. It's fulfilled humanity. It's authentic happiness.

Said differently, then, what is Jesus' way for living into the ultimate desire of the human heart? How do we become humanely happy?

At the beginning of his public movement, Jesus announced this way to an unlikely crowd of people. They were people familiar with physical suffering and mental illness. They came from different places and clashing cultures. Almost all of them were subjects and survivors of Rome's violent empire. James Baldwin called them a collection of "disreputable" and "improbable" people.[2]

Jesus spoke eight blessings to these people, each accompanied by a promise. I find whom Jesus blesses and what he promises them downright brilliant and beautiful. Before anything else, this is what Jesus wants to say to us—his strange wisdom for how to become human. When he says "blessed," he's really saying *happy*.

That's what the Beatitudinal Way is: Jesus' invitation to become humanely happy. Like Moses before him, he climbed a mountain on the outskirts of the empire. And like the rabbis of his time, he sat down and compressed his teaching into a compact "way." It's a fresh imagination and set of practices for becoming

---

2 Baldwin, 312.

our best selves, together, in our world, now and always.

Why Care?

Before commencing this quest, I want to ask a more basic question: why care about what Jesus taught 2,000 years ago?

Perhaps you already care and find Jesus' teaching compelling. Perhaps you don't and feel allergic simply reading the name "Jesus." Either way, you're welcome here. I believe there are good reasons for all of us to be curious about his Beatitudinal Way, whoever we are. Perhaps even reasons to allow his words more room in our lives.

Four are especially important to me.

First, Jesus practiced radical compassion. He was infamous for befriending the most othered people in his society: foreigners, abused women, addicts, the demonized and mentally ill, sufferers, the enslaved, and survivors of genocide. You wouldn't catch Socrates, Aristotle, or Seneca—the giants of Greco-Roman culture—in the company of these people. But Jesus made this love his way of life.

In fact, Jesus was the first person in history to teach, "Love your enemies." He taught this divergent love because of his beautiful vision of God. "God is kind to the ungrateful and wicked," he said. Jesus lived and taught this compassion, not in privilege and security, but in a hyper-polarized society, not too unlike our own today. Jesus was familiar with public executions, bloody insurrections, and devastating wars.

As we'll see, compassion is woven throughout his Beatitudinal Way.

Second, Jesus was fiercely critical of religious hypocrisy. For all of his compassion (or *because* of it), he didn't accept religion that othered people. By this I mean religion that sees "others" as unrelated or less than ourselves.

The Temple in Jerusalem—the holiest place on earth in Jesus' culture—had a sign on its gate that excluded foreigners. It threatened death if they tried to enter. Getting on this exclusive bandwagon was Jesus' ticket to power.

But Jesus had no appetite for toxic spiritual tricks. He literally turned the tables on this powerful establishment. His harshest critiques were reserved for the religious leaders who guarded it. He told them, "You shut the door of the kingdom of heaven in people's faces," when Jesus' desire was to swing this door wide open (Matthew 23:13). (To steal some thunder, "the kingdom of heaven" is Jesus' way of naming our unconditional belovedness and belonging.)

Jesus' critique of his own religion is fiercely and beautifully reflected in his Beatitudinal Way.

Third, Jesus had real integrity, not flashy words and flaky practice like so many spiritual entrepreneurs, then and now. He was willing to be rejected and to pay the ultimate price for this way of becoming humanely happy. In fact, he went all the way to public execution for it. But as we'll see, Jesus' compassion didn't crumble under this excruciating pressure.

The Beatitudinal Way that Jesus taught guides us into this rare integrity. We have precious wisdom to learn from a trauma survivor who was so free of resentment and able to remain creative amidst high-conflict.

Fourth, Jesus started the most successful social movement in human history. Despite being executed by the Empire, his movement has outlived Rome's oppression and implosion by 1,500 years.

No one would have believed this was possible when Jesus hung dying on a Roman lynching tree outside occupied Jerusalem.

But now we take for granted that billions of humans all over the earth—however confused and conflicted we may be—find inspiration in Jesus' movement.

The Beatitudinal Way is the roadmap of Jesus' movement. Howard Thurman, spiritual mentor of Martin Luther King Jr., beautifully captured the heart of it:

> "Christianity as it was born in the mind of this Jewish teacher and thinker appears as a technique of survival for the oppressed. That it became, through the intervening years, a religion of the powerful and the dominant, used sometimes as an instrument of oppression, must not tempt us into believing that it was thus in the mind and life of Jesus. 'In him was life, and this life was the light of humanity.' Wherever this spirit appears, the oppressed gather fresh courage; for he announced the good news that fear, hypocrisy, and hatred, the three hounds of hell that track the trail of the disinherited, need have no dominion over them."[3]

Whether you believe Jesus is the embodiment of God or simply a brilliant spiritual guide, he has sacred wisdom to teach all of us about how to become humanely happy. His radical compassion, religious critique, real integrity, and historic generativity compel us to ask, "What is the Beatitudinal Way?" How does Jesus invite us to flourish in the face of our universal experiences of suffering, conflict, and loss?

As we prepare for this journey, let me offer three further points of orientation.

---

3   Howard Thurman, *Jesus and the Disinherited* (Boston, MA: Beacon Press, 1996), 18-19.

Brilliant Design

First, as I'll show, each of Jesus' eight blessings builds on the previous one and integrates into a coherent, compelling way of life. Growing up, Jesus was a craftsman by trade, and he understood the importance of intentional design. Between each *beatus* is an insightful but unspoken linkage. These are not random well-wishes as we often seem to assume. Jesus is blueprinting an interconnected path and premeditated process of becoming human.

Each blessing is accompanied by a promise that speaks to a core fear we face in choosing to walk this way. The whole path reflects Jesus' deep sensitivity to the embodied human soul. He's intimately attuned to what we experience, what we fear, and what we need to be happy. In short, the Beatitudinal Way is more complex and challenging—more interesting and integrated—than we often imagine.

We might think of each blessing as a way-station. A way-station is important in its own right, but it also points to the next step of our journey. There's a *direction* here to understand and actively reorient our lives around. The ending, like the beginning, is unexpected, honest, and ultimately liberating.

As we travel from blessing to blessing, we become changed people who are coming home to Jesus' way of humane happiness.

Existential Decision

Second, I believe there's an unspoken moment of decision hovering between each of Jesus' eight blessings. As we navigate his way-stations and receive his promises, we face critical questions that confront our fears. With each one, the choice is ours for how we'll proceed.

The ancient rabbis described the silences of teachers and the blank spaces in their texts as "white fire." These are the open, oxygenating places between the logs where their teaching burns hottest and clearest. As the poet Judy Brown wrote:

> A fire
> grows
> simply because the space is there,
> with openings
> in which the flame
> that knows just how it wants to burn
> can find its way.[4]

I observe this pattern in Jesus' Beatitudinal Way.

In the open spaces between his blessings, fire meets us, and our humanity finds just how it wants to burn when we're coming truly alive.

At the end of each chapter, I'll highlight this subtle moment of decision, this crisis point, where we choose whether to continue our beatitudinal becoming or surrender to our fear.

A Roadmap for the Way

Before diving in, it might be helpful to sketch a brief overview of the path. I summarize this into a simple chart in Appendix 2 at the end of this book.

You may notice that I translate a few of Jesus' words slightly differently than the traditional rendering some of us have memorized. I believe these translations accurately capture what Jesus meant and invite us into a more expansive understanding of his Way.

1. Blessed are the poor in spirit, because theirs is the kingdom of heaven.

Jesus begins his Beatitudinal Way by naming our universal

---

4 Judy Brown, "Fire," in *The Sea Accepts All Rivers* (Bloomington, IA: Trafford, 2016), 34. I'm grateful to my friend Jason Ferenczi for sharing this poem with me.

human condition: *poverty*. And he speaks *blessing* to us poor people.

The truth is, all of us are poor in our own ways. But not all of us recognize our poverty or can receive our belovedness in the midst of its pain. We fear that our poverty is permanent. And so, we easily become hardened, grasp after invulnerability, and resist processing our suffering.

Will we stop here? Jesus promises us a new future of everlasting belovedness and invites us onward with his next blessing.

2. *Blessed are the grieving, because they will be comforted.*

Jesus next invites us into our grief and blesses us here.

Many of us fear that if we allow ourselves to grieve the pain of our poverty we'll come undone, become unwanted, and find ourselves abandoned. We feel pressured to appear healthy, happy, and successful.

But Jesus gives us permission to enter into the convulsive emotions of our experience and to process the pain that lives in us. We can be softened with our tears.

Still, grief can become intoxicating and boil into rage, vengeance, and violence. We easily try to overcome our pain by painishing others. (As I'll note again, "pain" is the root word of "punish.")

Will we stop here? Jesus promises us comfort and invites us onward with his next blessing.

3. *Blessed are the nonviolent, because they will inherit the earth.*

Jesus next calls us into nonviolence and blesses us in this practice.

Creative resistance to violence is one of Jesus' most groundbreaking teachings. Gandhi, who began each day by meditating on Jesus' words, wrote, "Jesus was the most active resister known perhaps to history. This was nonviolence par excellence."[5] Jesus' nonviolence is fierce but refuses to overcome poverty and grief by impoverishing and grieving others.

Of course, it also makes us more vulnerable and arouses our anxiety. Perhaps the greatest fear of the nonviolent is being endlessly displaced and dominated by the violent. And so, the nonviolent easily withdraw from the world and passively resign themselves to wait for a magic fix in a nebulous future.

Will we stop here? Jesus promises us that the whole world will become a home for the nonviolent and invites us onward with his next blessing.

4. Blessed are the hungry and thirsty for justice, because they will be filled.

Jesus next blesses those who passionately ache for right relationships of mutual flourishing. These people plunge into reimagining human identity, money, and power. They devote themselves to struggling for practical transformation, here and now.

But justice is also risky business. Allowing ourselves to long for a better world opens us to disappointment and the fear of being starved. Hope is dangerous.

If we're not careful, our craving for change easily consumes us and becomes judgmental condemnation. Before we know it, we find ourselves imitating the punishing patterns of injustice that we claim to be struggling to overcome.

Will we stop here? Jesus promises us that the justice-starved will be fully fed and invites us onward with his next blessing.

5. Blessed are the compassionate, because they will be mirrored with compassion.

Jesus next blesses those who open the aperture of their

---

5   Mahatma Gandhi, *Gandhi: On Nonviolence*, ed. Thomas Merton (New York, NY: New Directions, 2007), 55.

souls to the pain of others. In compassion, our craving for change expands into a universal mercy for all who suffer. Rather than condemnation, we learn afresh to desire our mutual flourishing.

But the fear of the compassionate is being unmirrored and left alone in our own pain. After opening ourselves to the misery of even our enemies, will we be abandoned and overwhelmed with the sadness? Cynicism easily sets in and shrouds our vision.

Will we stop here? Jesus promises us that the compassionate will be mirrored with compassion and invites us onward with his next blessing.

6. Blessed are the cleanhearted, because they will see God.

Jesus next blesses the cleanhearted. Immersing ourselves in the humbling waters of compassion cleanses the soul. Any lingering residue of superiority to others is slowly washed away. Notice that this sixth way-station is the first place that Jesus names *God*.

Still, this purifying baptism can feel like drowning. Plunged in the pain, we fear that we will never be able to see God or goodness again. Through the dark night of the soul, Jesus assures us that a heavenly vision will open, and we will hear the God of peace call us beloved.

But when this happens, we so often build a shrine to our religion. Our temptation is to camp out in catching a glimpse of God. We erect a wall around this holy revelation.

Will we stop here? Jesus daringly promises us divine vision but invites us still onward with his next blessing.

7. Blessed are the peacemakers, because they will be called children of God.

Jesus next blesses the peacemakers. We see in this seventh way-station that any authentic vision of God must open our eyes to perceive all people as our sacred siblings, including our enemies.

For Jesus, this is because of who *God* is. God is *our* Parent, as Jesus taught us to pray, and so peacemaking is our divine DNA. People of peace make healing relationships, reconciling communities, and overcoming othering our life's work, our divine family business.

But peacemaking is rarely popular. As we begin making peace, we fear being labeled as radicals and rejected as traitors. All too easily, we surrender to societal pressure and protect our approval at the price of peace.

Will we stop here? Jesus promises us that peacemakers will be correctly identified as God's children and invites us onward with his final blessing.

8. Blessed are the persecuted for the sake of justice, because theirs is the kingdom of heaven.

Jesus' Beatitudinal Way builds toward a brilliant but counter-intuitive climax: he speaks his final blessing to people who are *persecuted* for the sake of justice.

We see now that the path Jesus invites us to walk decisively deconforms us to the prevailing patterns of culture. It changes us. Beatitudinal humans have patiently traversed the previous seven way-stations, and so they count the cost of becoming *humanely* happy.

In the face of character assassination, exclusion, and killing, they remain courageously committed to truth, love, and justice. Jesus says that *these* persecuted people have become *prophets*. They unveil reality and reveal what is truly precious. To them, he declares at last, "Rejoice and be happy!"

But the fear of the persecuted is precisely the same as the poor: will we be insecure and suffer forever? Is there any hope or only permanent displacement?

Here Jesus promises us that the persecuted will be safe and perfectly at home in the kingdom of heaven without end.

And so, at last, Jesus invites us to begin again, to return to our first work and walk once more through our poverty, our grief, our nonviolence, and the rest of his Beatitudinal Way. This is the fiery path that takes us home—to the kingdom of heaven where our humanity wants to burn with true happiness forever.

The Rub

I want to stop here and launch into our journey. But I need to add one final point of orientation. Thanks for your patience.

From just a short overview of Jesus' Beatitudinal Way, we can see that he announced these blessings as a courageous critique and creative alternative to Moses' beatific way of becoming human.

Centuries before Jesus, Moses constituted a new nation named Israel. He did this, in part, by climbing up on a mountain and speaking blessings to his community. These blessings named what the people should expect if they chose to walk in God's way, what Moses called the Torah. This was his path and promise of Israelite happiness.

As we've seen, Jesus did exactly the same thing. He began his movement by climbing a mountain, speaking blessings, and inviting people into his Beatitudinal Way—his Torah. But Jesus daringly deviated from Moses' path, virtually from beginning to end.

Here's the rub.

Moses' blessings are strikingly similar to how we often imagine being "blessed" today. They center around being healthy, wealthy, triumphant, and divinely favored over "others." This is how he described them:

> "You will be blessed more than any other people. None of your men or women will be childless, nor will any of your livestock be without young. The Lord will keep you free from

every disease. He will not inflict on you the horrible diseases you knew in Egypt, but he will inflict them on all your enemies. You must destroy all the peoples the Lord your God gives over to you. Do not look on them with compassion...

The Lord will open the heavens, the storehouse of his bounty, to send rain on your land in season and to bless all the work of your hands. You will lend to many nations but will borrow from none. The Lord will make you the head, not the tail. If you pay attention to the commands of the Lord your God that I give you this day and carefully follow them, you will always be at the top, never at the bottom. God will be an enemy to your enemies."[6] (Deuteronomy 7:14-16; 28:12-13; Exodus 23:22-26)

Sounds familiar, doesn't it?

Notice that Moses offers Israel an inherently othering vision of blessing: "*You* will be blessed *more* than any *other* people." This mindset entrenches comparison and competition within and between people. It makes "others" appear unrelated or less than ourselves.

Of course, Moses' Torah includes groundbreaking moral teachings that enshrine universal human dignity, security, and justice as the very heart of God. Moses introduced the revolutionary command, "Love your neighbor as yourself." The Bible is a richly complex book with many layers and numerous voices, which are in spirited dialogue—sometimes *fierce* dialogue—with one another. Jesus joins and expands this dialogue with his Beatitudinal Way.

---

6 Moses' teaching connected murderous, mass violence and God's blessing in other places as well. See Exodus 32:28-29: "The Levites did as Moses commanded [killing their apostate brothers, friends, and neighbors], and that day about three thousand of the people died. Then Moses said, 'You have been set apart to the Lord today, for you were against your sons and brothers, and he has blessed you this day.'"

But in the crucial passages I just quoted, the sacrosanct goal is *supremacy*. Your family will be fertile. Your fields will be fruitful. Your enemies will be *God's* foes. And you will fight and win your wars against them.

This vision becomes the foundation for Moses' religious nationalism. By this I mean the nation's claim to being exclusively chosen, exceptional, and superior to "others." Today, this perspective and project is often referred to as "Zionism," though that term has a complex history rich with fierce debate like the Bible itself.[7]

With this othering identity, Moses tells Israel to commit genocide against "all" the indigenous women, children, and men of the land. He repeatedly warns them to allow "no survivors." His supremacist mandate criminalizes compassion. Simply seeing others with mercy becomes a blasphemous temptation to be

---

7   Zionism is a complex term that is used in different ways in different contexts. As Professor David Gushee kindly wrote to me, "19th and early 20th century Zionism was a largely secular Jewish movement to press for a return of Jews to their ancient homeland—based on the conclusion that Jews like other peoples needed such a homeland for their own self-determination, security, and dignity... Prophetic Jewish figures like Martin Buber were concerned after 1945 that Jews not lose the lessons of their long biblical legacy as well as their suffering in diaspora. They wanted to nurture a new nation that would not be a bully or misuse its power."

In this book, when I refer to "Zionism," I have in mind the supremacist perspective and project that pits Israel's dignity and security against its neighbors, especially Palestinians. More broadly, Christian Zionism has a powerful influence in majority-Christian countries like Russia, Ethiopia, and the United States.

Note well: critiquing the supremacist strand of Zionism and Zionistic aspects of Moses' teaching is *not* the same as affirming antisemitism or denying that Jewish people have a right to a secure home, especially in light of the genocidal horror of the Holocaust, which I explore in this book. Jews have been some of the strongest critics of Zionism, insisting that asserting special status for one's own group is morally corrupting and produces enmity, insecurity, and conflict.

Antisemitism is a grave evil that has plagued the Christian tradition, often fueled by the supremacist notion of "Christian supersessionism." All followers of Jesus must condemn and oppose this. Jesus was Jewish, built his Beatitudinal Way on the foundation of Hebrew Scripture, and calls us to love *all* others as our neighbors, including Jews, Palestinians, and, indeed, Zionists. My perspective on the Holy Land has been deeply influenced by the Telos Group and can be summarized as pro-Israeli, pro-Palestinian, pro-peace.

For a study of modern Zionism, see Walter Laqueur, *A History of Zionism: From the French Revolution to the Establishment of the State of Israel* (New York, NY: Knopf Doubleday, 2003). For a study of antisemitism in Christian history, see William Nicholls, *Christian Antisemitism: A History of Hate* (Lanham, MD: Rowman & Littlefield, 1995).

crushed with violence. "God" and genocide gel.[8]

(If you're thinking, "Wait a second! I thought Andrew believed in the Bible!" kindly read Appendix 3 at the end of this book. I unpack my understanding of inspired Scripture there.)

Jesus' divergence from Moses is what makes his Beatitudinal Way so much more than a comforting personal journey. It's also culturally critical and prophetically political. Recognizing this is crucial. It gives us the key to understanding why the religious and political leaders of Jesus' society saw him as a dangerous threat who was ultimately worthy of execution.

Acknowledging this divergence is still spectacularly unpopular and piously punished today. I expect this aspect of my book to be most challenging to some readers. Still, I believe it's undeniable and urgent to face. We can't avoid this truth if we're going to become *humanely* happy and avoid the cycle of catastrophe.

James Baldwin named what's at stake with fearless clarity:

"I think that the past is all that makes the present coherent and further, the past will remain horrible for exactly as long as we refuse to assess it honestly... People who shut their eyes to reality simply invite their own destruction, and

---

8　When I refer to genocide in this book, I have in mind the definition used by the United States Holocaust Memorial Museum: "Genocide is an internationally recognized crime where acts are committed with the intent to destroy, in whole or in part, a national, ethnic, racial, or religious group." See "What Is Genocide" at www.ushmm.org.

If you consider it inaccurate or excessive to call biblical violence "genocide," kindly review the definition of genocide above and the following biblical texts: Deuteronomy 2:34; 3:6; 6:10-11; Joshua 6:21; 8:22-25; 24:12-13; 1 Samuel 15:2; 27:9; 2 Samuel 8:2; Esther 8:17 and 9:12-16.

The misuse of God's name for human purposes provoked Jewish writers to start referring to God as G-d. As I wrote in my previous book, "This hallowing practice disruptively reminds humans that all of our sayings of God are hollow. God is never captured by our language or power. The true G-d is always both less and more than we believe—breaking out of our boxes, slipping through our spellings, opening space for the suffering, and crying out for their freedom." See *Flourishing on the Edge of Faith: Seven Practices for a New We* (Washington, DC: BitterSweet Collective, 2022), 33.

anyone who insists on remaining in a state of innocence long after that innocence is dead turns himself into a monster... The great force of history comes from the fact that we carry it within us, are unconsciously controlled by it in many ways, and history is literally present in all that we do."[9]

Baldwin said this more simply: "we have to look grim facts in the face because if we don't, we can never hope to change them."[10]

Here are the grim facts: Moses' supremacist vision of blessing is a blueprint of today's prosperity gospel and religious nationalism rolled into one. It remains wildly popular around the world and makes a lot of sense in the face of the human condition.

We're all insecure. We all suffer. And we all want to be healthy, wealthy, and win. I do too. Baldwin said it bluntly: "Men have an enormous need to debase other men."[11] Claiming that "God" promises us these "blessings" constructs an iron dome against our consciences asking inconvenient questions: "But what if we were them? What if we are *them*? What if we are *we*?"

Devout Jews knew Moses' way of mountaintop blessing by heart. Their longing for it to be fulfilled was radicalized under the brutal military occupation of the Roman Empire. Around the time that Jesus launched the Beatitudinal Way, the colonizers had publicly executed 2,000 people. This was their 9/11 or October 7th—a horrifying spectacle of political terrorism.

So, when this gifted teacher gathered a large crowd on a mountainside and began to declare blessings, they knew the script. They likely expected—and almost certainly *wanted*—Jesus to say, "If you follow me, God will make you healthy, wealthy, and

---

9 James Baldwin, *James Baldwin: Collected Essays*, ed. Toni Morrison (New York, New York: The Library of America, 1998), 7, 21, 22, 119, 129, 723.

10 Baldwin, 216.

11 Baldwin, 216.

triumphant over your enemies. You can tell who's blessed by who looks like *that*."

But Jesus teaches a different way of blessing that amounts to a radical abolition of the old beaten path. Here at the trailhead to his movement, he invites a crowd of wildly diverse people into a new way of becoming *humanely* happy. He doesn't speak of being "more blessed" or superior to anyone else. There isn't a hint of prosperity ideology or religious nationalism over "enemies." No canceling of compassion. No condition for genocide.

Divergent.

Each of Jesus' blessings and the fire between them burns away our othering addictions. Jesus invites us to learn an ancient yet innovative Torah into humane happiness.

No wonder the people were in awe when Jesus finished this teaching. They said that he taught with a strange, new *authority*. His way was unlike anything they'd ever heard before from the traditional guardians of Zion (Matthew 7:28-29).

And they were right: the heart of what Jesus said in this teaching was fresh and surprising in ancient religion. Bittersweetly, it remains so for us still today. No doubt, I've already written enough to make some readers assume I've lost my way.

Read on if the fire burns in you.

***

Over half my life ago, I remember telling Jesus that I wanted to be more "blessable." I wasn't asking to be "more blessed" than anyone else. I wanted to live more deeply into the way he mapped in this teaching. His path felt foreign to me, even as I had memorized his words as a child.

Looking back, I think my prayer was actually answered. But as I indicated in my opening letter, I've found its ongoing fulfillment far more painful than I had guessed. Entering into Jesus' Beatitudinal Way has been unsettling. Sometimes seemingly unbearable. It begins and ends in radical vulnerability.

But I've also found that this blessed way is actually deconforming and changing me. It isn't just conveniently confirming what I thought I already knew. It's enlarging my humanity. It's transforming me into a person that I know I want to become, even across the unhappy experiences I narrated from 2023. The Beatitudinal Way is an endlessly generative, culturally divergent path to humane happiness.

I'm slowly learning to trust it. In my gut, I know this is the way.

So, what is the Beatitudinal Way of Jesus?

It starts in the most universal yet unwanted experience of our humanity. Buckle up. Or don't.

Allow yourself to be as you really are. This is where Jesus' path begins and the only way we can walk it to the end. As Baldwin wrote, "Our humanity is our burden, our life; we need not battle for it; we need only to do what is infinitely more difficult—that is, to accept it."[12]

---

12 Baldwin, *Collected Essays*, 18.

CHAPTER 3

Way-Station 1: Poverty

For Precious: Thank you
for showing me the poor are precious.

"Lucky are the unlucky."
Philip Yancey[1]

---

1 Philip Yancey, *The Jesus I Never Knew* (Grand Rapids, MI: Zondervan, 1995), 105.

Precious' House

When I think of poverty, I'm transported to the old house of my friend Precious.

Precious and I met on the streets of Addis Ababa when she was selling packs of tissues and sticks of gum after dark. She was barely ten years old at the time. In the shadows of the shiny new buildings on Africa Avenue, I'd often hear her clanky cane before I'd see her bright, kind eyes.

Precious was a typical kid. She loved swimming, running, and flinging her body into cartwheels. But her young bones were battered by tuberculosis. After her family left their rural home to find help in the capital city, a doctor gave Precious the wrong injection. He said the feeling in her legs would return. But it never really did. There was no going back.

So Precious hobbled along the main strip in Addis until late at night trying to help her family survive. One hand clutched her cane; the other balanced a piece of cardboard with a spread of tissues and gum. She looked like an absurd, half-pint waitress. Poverty means you work—even if you're ten, disabled, and defenseless in the dark.

It turns out that Precious and I lived in adjacent neighborhoods. Our paths often crossed, so we'd share bread-and-banana dinners on the street as I walked home from work. With time, I asked Precious if I could meet her family and learn more about their story.

Itash was Precious' loving mother, the obvious source of her kind eyes. After vetting me on Africa Avenue, she led me on a long hike to their hidden home.

Precious' family lived at the bottom of a muddy hill next to a filthy river in the bowels of a nearby slum. When it rained, the path turned into a treacherous flow of fecal muck. Still, Precious always managed the slope with her cane and halting shuffle.

This was her new childhood acrobatics after disease and poverty vandalized her body.

We hiked down the hill, weaved through a jumble of large rocks, and finally descended into the clearing where they lived with five other families. Their mini-neighborhood felt more like the bottom of a pit. Roasted coffee, ground chili pepper, and raw sewage wafted through the air.

Precious' house, like the others, was a stick-framed, mud-spackled shack with a slab of sheet metal on top. Roughly ten-by-ten, this single room was home for two adults and five children: Precious, her mom, her dad, her three younger siblings, and her cousin Lazarus whom they'd adopted when his mom had a mental breakdown.

A tarp served as their floor. One hard mattress provided bedding for their seven bodies. A wood-slab bench sat beside the bed as their couch. Their four mud walls were hung with scraps of Dell Computer boxes to insulate them against Addis' biting wind. (Precious' dad—a soft-spoken, resilient, gently dignified man—was emaciated from HIV/AIDS. Even a common cold could prove deadly.) Paper icons of Jesus were taped to the boxes as their only art.

This shack was their home and all they had. Except they didn't even *have* this. After Precious' medical needs drove them to the city, they squatted illegally on this postage stamp of dirt that they couldn't afford to own. Eviction was a constant threat, which they narrowly escaped more than once.

On that first day of our friendship, Itash generously welcomed me as a total stranger. She brewed me coffee and prepared a plate full of her fresh-baked injera. She has done this for me, my students, and my friends countless times across the years ever since.

Precious' home is a portrait of poverty and what it can be like to be poor. The space is small, unbeautiful, and woefully inadequate. It shelters a painful story punctuated with tragedy, trauma, and suffering. A riddled sense of ever-present precarity and inescapable permanence battle against one another day after day. Vulnerability pervades, even as love burns inside.

I share this small part of her family's story with their permission. It is *not* meant to define them but to illustrate the reality behind Jesus' first blessing on the poor. Precious, Itash, and their beautiful family became my teachers of the Beatitudinal Way.

Some people may see emptiness and insignificance in this slum. Some may even see shame, inferiority, or worthlessness. No doubt, the people living here struggle with these degrading impressions, from without and within.

If the river floods, or a resentful neighbor starts a fire, or the government sends a bulldozer, would anyone even remember they were here? Would anyone grieve their absence?

Jesus' First Blessing

This is where Jesus begins his Beatitudinal Way: with the poor in the bowels of human suffering. This is his primal blessing for that wildly divergent crowd and all of us still searching for happiness today: *Blessed are the poor in spirit, because theirs is the kingdom of heaven.*

What a strange starting point for a movement. It reveals Jesus' heart and the most basic orientation of his way of becoming humanely happy.

Jesus begins by speaking dignity to the degraded and love for the vulnerable. He says that if you've suffered deprivation and devastation—if your life is familiar with pain, precarity, and loss—you're not abandoned or inferior. God sees you. God wants you. And God won't discard you or let you disappear into nothingness.

You're not cheap. You're precious, just like my friend and her dear family, despite so many appearances to the contrary.

Perhaps the core fear of the poor is that their poverty is permanent. But Jesus promises us that it won't go on forever. No, when the story ends, we'll be perfectly safe and permanently at home with God. In fact, God promises us an everlasting belovedness and belonging that's more beautiful than we can presently imagine: the kingdom of heaven. (Try to keep this in mind for chapter six.) As the medieval mystic Meister Eckhart wrote, "God loves us with the very same love by which God loves and cherishes Godself... God loves us in such a way that it is as if God's blessedness depends on it."[2]

In short, a sovereign goodness is the destiny of the poor. It's where our story ends—and begins again without end. The unlucky, the losers, the groaning nobodies who feel obsolete at the bottom of the pit—they're *blessed* and promised undying *happiness*.

Defiantly, Jesus spoke this blessing out of his own experience of being a poor person. His family was forced to relocate by the empire. Then his mother Mary delivered him in an animal shelter among fecal muck.

Soon after, Jesus' family narrowly escaped a political massacre. Like millions of other poor people, then and now, they became refugees. God only knows how many times Jesus nursed at Mary's breast with her tears washing over him. The heightened stress chemicals in her milk seeped into his neurobiology from his earliest days.

Jesus then grew up in an obscure village as a manual laborer under Rome's brutal imperial occupation. Executed bodies and the ache of humiliation littered the landscape and soulscape of

---

2 Meister Eckhart, *Meister Eckhart: The Essential Sermons, Commentaries, Treatises and Defense* (Classics of Western Spirituality), trans. Bernard McGinn (Mahwah, NJ: Paulist Press, 1981).

Jesus' short, everyday life. He was born poor and died poor.

No wonder Jesus understood that poverty takes various forms on a complex spectrum. It can look like the material poverty and oppression that Precious' family, Jesus' family, and so many of us endure (Luke 6:20). It also includes the existential, inner destitution that often haunts many people like me who pass as privileged (Matthew 5:3).

Spanning this spectrum, the word Jesus uses for "poor" literally means one who crouches or cowers, one who is bent down and beggarly. It's the cringe that creeps into our consciousness and tries to cripple our humanity when the birthright of our dignity is vandalized.

When Jesus blesses the "poor in spirit," then, he's speaking to people who feel overwhelmed with their own humiliating smallness. They ache with emptiness and groan with disappointment. They know the gnawing feeling of being weak, inadequate, not-enough in the vital center of their life—their spirit, their agency, their very breath (*pneuma*). They inhabit—or feel like they *embody*—a small shack in the bowels of a slum with disease and insecurity clinging to the air. No doubt, Jesus is speaking to the traumatized, the depressed, the mentally sick, the suicidal, the people whose will to live is withering away. The *poor* in *spirit*.

It's to *these* seemingly redundant people that Jesus announces his first blessing. The Beatitudinal Way doesn't begin with the healthy, the wealthy, and the winning. It starts when we find ourselves suffering, lacking, needing—afflicted with all the signs of being inferior, insufficient, and *un*blessed down at the mucking bottom.

Jesus doesn't explain this. He *announces* it. And the fact that he announces it out of *his own* poverty is what gives it credibility to me. If you're poor—in body, spirit, or otherwise—God is unconditionally committed to you. If you feel like you're falling apart or there's nothing left to live for but pain, you will end up fully at home with God. If you're hopeless, you're held by heaven. You're going to be eternally okay. The precarity that feels permanent and all-too pervasive isn't unimpeachable. The ending is good. You're safe forever.

Yours is the kingdom of heaven.

The Human Condition

The first way-station of Jesus' path perceives the human condition with profound insight and universality, whoever and wherever we are.

The truth is, we all start poor. We can't walk. Can't talk. Can't feed, clean, or protect ourselves. We're completely vulnerable, absolutely dependent on others for *everything*. If we were alone, we'd wither away and die—or survive as shadows of who we're meant to be.

Equally so, we all end poor, whoever else we might have been. Our hair grays and falls out. Our bodies droop and decay. We lose our memories and minds. Relationships thin. People die; we die. *Everyone dies.* However and whenever this happens, the end of our earthly journey is a guaranteed return to our universal beginning: poverty. This is perhaps our one certainty in life.

Between birth and death, our humanity is pervaded by ever-present vulnerability and astonishing fragility. We're utterly dependent on air, water, food, shelter, and functioning organs simply to survive. This doesn't touch our fundamental needs for love, dignity, and hope. Many of us are starved for relationship, even if we're surrounded by people in the prime of our lives.

We experience loneliness, stress, disappointment, betrayal, abandonment, and anxiety. We battle depression, addiction, and a gnawing sense that our life is empty of meaning. Slums spread within us and about us. We lack what we need but can't figure out how to get it. Often enough, we can't even figure out what *it* is.

We experience conflict, suffer violence, carry trauma, lose

loved ones, and ache with pain in our relationships, personally and politically. The toxic chemistry lab of shame, fear, anger, resentment, rage, and hate spills within our bodies and between our bodies—confusing, scarring, and separating us. Unforeseen events alter or end our lives in a heartbeat. We reel as our world suddenly comes underdone and everything changes. I certainly do, as I described in my opening letter.

This is our bitter(sweet) truth from start to finish: all of us are poor in spirit. Whether this manifests materially or not. Whether we acknowledge it or not. Whether we think we've overcome it or not. We are these natal, mortal, fragile creatures. One way or another, no one escapes being poor.

Jesus meets us in this discomforting reality and speaks his first blessing to us: *Blessed are the poor in spirit, because theirs is the kingdom of heaven.*

If you're part of this human condition, God holds you close. If you've lost whatever you think makes life worth living, God still wants you. If you've been stripped of everything that could make you stand out or stand above someone else, there's a home for you. You will be perfectly safe in the everlasting belovedness and belonging of God.

This is Jesus' first, foundational blessing at the beginning of his movement. It's the gateway to everything else he wants to say to us about becoming humanely happy.

To me, it's either the cruelest mockery or the most comforting promise for everyone everywhere always: the poor are precious to God. They—*we*—are wanted and welcomed by heaven forever.[3]

---

3 Notice that Jesus doesn't bless poverty itself or say, "You're blessed because you're poor." Jesus isn't a masochist who takes pleasure in pain. He blesses poor people and says they're destined to be perfectly at home in God's future. As I'll say again, I suspect that Jesus begins by blessing the poor for several reasons. First, they're the people we often assume are unblessed or even cursed, and Jesus wants to abolish this assumption. Second, the poor really are all of us, and so this blessing can speak to everyone, if we're willing to receive it. Third, the vulnerability of poverty may be a condition in which radical transformation becomes possible in our lives; it can be the beginning of a longer, life-changing journey.

James Baldwin—the grandson of an enslaved woman, a survivor of sexual abuse, and a Black man in white supremacist America—was surely right: "Life would scarcely be bearable if this hope did not exist."[4]

Crisis 1: Hardness or Grief?

This takes us to our first moment of decision, our first *crisis*, on Jesus' Beatitudinal Way: What will we do with the pain of our poverty?

There's no doubt about it: all poverty is painful. It can be excruciating and terribly traumatizing. But what will we do with it? Will we allow our pain to harden us?

All too easily, suffering strips us of tenderness and drives us away from vulnerability. We fear that our poverty is permanent, and so we chase after armored appearances of happiness defined as health, wealth, and winning. If only deep down inside, we try to surmount that dreadful feeling of being less by making ourselves *more* than someone else. Before we know it, we pass along our pain.

This is how poverty is often perpetuated. We poor people avoid processing our pain and impoverish others. This can take all sorts of forms: religious, psychological, sexual, cultural, economic, political—you name it. But the tragedy is that we frequently impoverish others in our desperate attempt to escape poverty ourselves.

We see this tragic plot play out in the story of Israel. The Hebrew people finally escaped 400 years of enslaved poverty in a genocidal empire. But then under Moses' leadership, they sought to establish their own supremacist identity.

As they did so, they tried to overcome their poverty by becoming "more blessed" than others. They unleashed genocidal violence against the indigenous people of the land. One poverty led

---

4 Baldwin, 126.

to another. Israel may have escaped the shadows of the Egyptian pyramids, but Israel rebuilt them in the religious-nationalist hierarchy of its own imagination.

In many ways, this is a universal pattern of our hurting humanity.

I see it in my own faith community. The early Christians were brutally persecuted by the Roman Empire. Still, Jesus' movement spread like wildfire because of its countercultural blessing for the poor.

But after 300 years, Christians began seizing imperial power for themselves and persecuting "the pagans." In 312 AD, Emperor Constantine took the cross, a symbol of Rome's murderous violence against its enemies, and "Christianized" it into the Roman military's logo. It became a kind of lucky charm for victory in battle.

Then in 330 AD, the powerful bishop Eusebius gave his famous "Oration in Praise of Constantine." In the presence of his "divinely favored emperor," the churchman declared, "God's friend, graced by his heavenly favor with victory over all his enemies, subdues and chastens the open adversaries of the truth in accordance with the usages of war." Not so subtly, Eusebius baptized holy war and outlined what we call "Christian nationalism" today.[5]

Centuries later, the tables turned again, and Christian minorities in Europe were persecuted by other Christians. They then fled as "pilgrims" across the Atlantic Ocean in search of a Promised Land. But when they arrived, they unleashed the violence of the old empire on the Native peoples of the "New World." Grievously, they committed genocide with their claim to

---

5 Philip Schaff, n.d. "Eusebius Pamphilius: Church History, Life of Constantine, Oration in Praise of Constantine." Christian Classics Ethereal Library. https://ccel.org/ccel/schaff/npnf201/npnf201. See sections 1:6, 2:3, 3:3, and 3:8.

"manifest destiny."[6]

Modern Israel has reproduced this supremacist pattern in Palestine since 1948.

But we can choose another path. We can process our pain and allow it to *soften* us.

Jesus' first blessing is an invitation into this strange, vulnerable road less traveled. He calls us to trust that we're cherished by God even in our poverty. We're precious to heaven precisely when we feel like we are nothing and have nothing over anyone else. Here ends othering.

Will we accept that we're accepted?

This trust can set our lives on a whole new trajectory. Here at ground zero, we begin a long journey of surrendering our need to be "more blessed" or "better" than anyone else. We let go and allow our suffering to perform a miracle: to open us and connect us to one another.

Instead of hardening ourselves and striving for superior appearances, we enter into the ultimate unionizer of humanity: *our grief.*

Etty Hillesum (1914-1943) documented this decision in her diary with rare profundity. Etty was a Dutch Jewish woman living in Nazi-occupied Amsterdam. Not long after starting to write, she would be deported to the Auschwitz concentration camp and be murdered at the tender age of twenty-nine.

Germany had recently lost World War I. It was desperately impoverished and humiliated. Out of this pain, Hitler rose to power

---

6 See David Stannard, *American Holocaust: The Conquest of the New World* (New York, NY: Oxford University Press, 1993); Roxanne Dunbar-Ortiz, *An Indigenous Peoples' History of the United States* (Boston, MA: Beacon Press, 2015); and Willie Jennings, *The Christian Imagination: Theology and the Origins of Race* (New Haven, CT: Yale University Press, 2011).

by promising Germans a new prosperity. He said this "Greater Germany" would be achieved through a "hard pedagogy," a new process of becoming human. Hitler described his way like this:

> "My pedagogy is hard. What is weak must be hammered away. In my fortresses of the Teutonic Order [a Christian military society], a young generation will grow up before which the world will tremble. I want the young to be violent, domineering, undismayed, cruel. The young must be all these things. They must be able to bear pain. There must be nothing weak or gentle about them."[7]

Soon enough, Germany's impoverished quest to be "great again" took the form of struggling for supremacy over Jews and other minorities. The outcome was predictable and catastrophic: poverty, genocide, and yet another world war. An estimated 73 million people died in the wake of this "pedagogy."

Etty understood the Nazis' genocidal intent. She wrote in her journal, "Life is going to be very hard. We shall be torn apart, all who are dear to one another."[8] This acute pain was anguishing. She prayed in her diary, "Dear God, today I cannot praise you, I honestly don't feel happy enough."[9] It wasn't only that she was "unhappy all the time," as she recorded feeling. Etty and her people were "more unhappy than ever before." She confessed, "There are days I can no longer carry on."[10]

Etty's journals are difficult to read. They describe an

7 Quoted in Jonathan Glover, *Humanity: A Moral History of the Twentieth Century*, second edition (New Haven, CT: Yale University Press, 2012), 337. Notice that Hitler sees gentleness as weakness rather than strength. This is a tell-tale sign of tyrants.

8 Etty Hillesum, *Etty Hillesum: An Interrupted Life and Letters from Westerbork*, trans. Arnold Pomerans (New York, NY: Henry Holt and Co., 1996), 88. I'm grateful to my wife Lily for introducing me to Etty's writing.

9 Hillesum, *An Interrupted Life*, 100.

10 Hillesum, *An Interrupted Life*, 141-142.

excruciating, ruthlessly imposed poverty. She wrote:

> "I have already died a thousand deaths in a thousand
> concentration camps... My body has disintegrated into
> a thousand pieces, and each piece has a different pain...
> [I feel like] a flood tide of despair, of elemental human
> sorrow... as if my face were withering and decaying before
> my very eyes, and as if everything were falling apart in
> front of me and my heart were letting everything go."[11]

It's difficult to imagine a more extreme poverty or more
radical pain. Etty's body, her spirit, her family, her society, her
sense of basic dignity, security, and hope—*everything* was being
stripped away.

And still, during this hellish nightmare, Etty was meditating
"morning and night"[12] on Jesus' Beatitudinal Way. You can feel its
influence in who she was becoming.

As she took stock of her life under Hitler's "hard pedagogy,"
this is how Etty defiantly defined authentic human maturity: "to
bear a great many hard things in life *and yet not to grow too hard
inside*."[13] She clarified what she meant later in her journal: "There is
a difference between hardy and hard. It is often forgotten nowadays.
I believe I get hardier every day... but I shall never grow hard."[14]

Paradoxically, Etty matured into hardiness by not
hardening herself. Instead, she relentlessly processed her poverty
and shamelessly poured out her pain.

Her journals endure as eloquent testament to this practice.

---

11 Hillesum, *An Interrupted Life*, 150-151, 166, 180.

12 Hillesum, *An Interrupted Life*, 108.

13 Hillesum, *An Interrupted Life*, 127.

14 Hillesum, *An Interrupted Life*, 195.

Rather than rage and enmity, the pages of her short life are saturated with honest grief and empathy for others. The pain of poverty led Etty to confession and connection—not to hardness and hostility. She became an emotionally honest person who could connect with seemingly everyone, as we'll see in the chapters to come.

I've observed a similar quality in Precious and her family with their paper icons of Jesus taped to their mud walls. Many times I've sat with Itash in her home as tears streamed down her face. She's also sat in my home as those same tears have streamed down my face. Poverty has taken this family through many hard times in the bowels of suffering.

But they haven't been hardened by poverty or closed their hearts to others. Their humble shanty is often packed with strangers who are welcomed with warm hospitality, just like I was. We find a home there, just like little Lazarus has.

Poverty is our universal condition, our crisis, and this is where Jesus begins his Beatitudinal Way: *Blessed are the poor in spirit, because theirs is the kingdom of heaven.* Jesus speaks divine dignity, security, and hope to the poor—*to all of us.* He declares that we're *blessed*, destined for heaven's everlasting home of unconditional belovedness and belonging. Even when we feel like we're nobody, we're still somebody to God and always will be.

But in the meantime, each of us faces this critical decision: Will we allow the pain of our poverty to harden us and send us down the beaten path of competition with one another? Or will we accept that we're accepted, process our pain, and be softened to one another by our shared grief?

This is the heart of Jesus' second blessing.

CHAPTER 4

Way-Station 2: Grief

For Anna: Thank you
for helping me befriend my tears.

"Grief must be witnessed to be healed."
Elisabeth Kübler-Ross[1]

---

1 Elisabeth Kübler-Ross and David Kessler, *On Grief and Grieving: Finding the Meaning of Grief Through the Five Stages of Loss* (New York, NY: Scribner, 2005), 63.

Step Through

I realize that it can be annoying to be told about a book you may not have read yet. But I need to start here. I trust you'll appreciate why in a moment.

At the beginning of Toni Morrison's Pulitzer Prize-winning novel *Beloved*, Paul D visits his old friend Sethe. They were among the survivors who escaped the violence of American slavery in the Deep South many years before. But the treacherous path to freedom had separated them, and they hadn't seen one another since.

Now wandering in Ohio, Paul D sits on Sethe's front porch and waits for her to come home from work. But as he waits, he discovers a secret: her house was haunted. It shook as red lights flashed ominously inside. The furniture moved. Indiscernible voices hissed through the window.

When Sethe finally gets home, she invites Paul D to come inside. But he's afraid and steps back from the door. He interrogates her: "What kind of evil you got in here?" Even after such a long journey, perhaps it'd be better to walk away and just keep wandering.

But Sethe replies, "It's not evil, just sad. Come on. Just step through."[2]

Morrison is inviting us to see something truly profound. We often experience our sadness as a frightful evil to be avoided at all cost. Our house shakes with flashing red lights. The floor moves. We hear threatening voices inside that we can't fully understand.

In response, we easily withdraw. We refuse to step foot into such a haunting house of volatile emotion. If we do move closer, we raise "heavy knives of defense against misery, regret, gall and hurt."[3] We harden ourselves.

---

2 Toni Morrison, *Beloved* (New York, NY: Knopf, 1987), 8.

3 Morrison, *Beloved*, 86.

But Sethe understands what's going on inside. The house's haunting is the undead suffering of her extreme poverty and broken heart. It reveals the trauma of injustice and the death of Beloved—Sethe's helpless baby girl who didn't survive the dangerous journey north to freedom.

The death of Beloved—what Morrison calls "the one word that matters"[4]—is the source of all our grief. It's what James Baldwin called the "shrieking grave," whether it's located in the earth or in our living bodies.[5]

Still, Sethe had started her grief work and calls out to Paul D: "It's not evil, just sad. Come on. Just step through... Anything dead coming back to life hurts."[6] And so he does, with "a wave of grief that soaked him so thoroughly he wanted to cry."[7]

In many ways, this is the invitation that Jesus whispers between "Blessed are the poor" and his next way-station "Blessed are the grieving": *It's not evil, just sad. Come on. Just step through... Anything dead coming back to life hurts.*

Allow yourself to enter the haunted house where grief clings to the air and is given permission to wash over you. Come in to the space where vulnerability and sorrow aren't banished but can express themselves freely. Be present in that frightful dwelling where defenses are put down and you dare to feel the range of what lives inside of you. Even if it hurts like hell and shakes the foundations of your life, just step through.

This is where the Beatitudinal Way of Jesus takes us next.

---

4 Morrison, *Beloved*, 5.

5 Baldwin, *Collected Essays*, 381.

6 Morrison, *Beloved*, 35.

7 Morrison, *Beloved*, 9.

Grief Work(s)

My house shook when I started "stepping through."

In the summer of 2019, I'd wake up early in the morning with a dull panic. I could barely breathe. It felt like someone was standing on my chest and crushing my lungs.

When I made it out of bed, anxiety raced through my body. It tingled in my left elbow, in my knee. I often found myself breathless and needing to *choose* to inhale.

Whenever I talked about something important and painful to me, water would start bursting out of my eyes. I felt like I had become an ocean of tears inside.

Wherever I was, with whomever I was, manic voices looped in my head and wouldn't turn off. They hounded me and insisted I was blocked, under pressure, afraid of everyone.

They were telling the truth. The engine of my life was overheating. I urgently needed to shut down.

During this time, I started sitting in silence and heard the unmistakable whisper: *Be silent and still.* But I was desperately afraid to do that—*to not do*. I feared that if I turned off the ignition and became still enough to face whatever this was inside of me, I'd never be able to turn on again. Would I be permanently broken down and disappoint everyone I love? Is it safe to process my pain?

My friend Andy Crouch introduced me to a spiritual director named Duane Grobman, and we started to talk. Duane was different from the charismatic spiritual leaders I was familiar with. He asked me to tell him my story and listened patiently without interruption.

When I finally stopped talking, Duane said something that took me by surprise. It was so obvious that I hadn't allowed myself to see it. He said, "Andrew, you've experienced a lot of loss and grief in your life."

I'm a middle-class, white, straight, American, Christian man. And I have friends like Precious. I've spent time in the haunted house of extreme poverty. So facing *my own* painful poverty felt like a guilty luxury. Something in me insisted that stepping through, as Morrison wrote, and coming home to my grief was shameful and self-indulgent. I was afraid to go back inside my shrieking shack of memories in which I felt helpless, humiliated, and overwhelmed with sadness.

And yet, I desperately needed to do this. I was suffocating. My beloved body was doing everything it could to tell me that I couldn't continue if I avoided this any longer. I had to step through, into my own haunted house, or become one of the undead myself.

Duane gave me homework. He asked me to sit in silence and list as many significant places of grief in my life as I could remember. I still recall where I was when I started my grief work: sitting on my bed, with my legs crossed, hunched over in that cringing posture of poverty.

The tears exploded from my eyes. They didn't stream down my face. They burst like shrapnel out of my soul.

Still, I sat in silence.
Then I began to write.
And then, I shook with weeping.

Then another grief presented itself. And I began to write again. And more tears exploded from my face as I shook.

Unpracticed in the grieving process, I assumed this would be a quick exercise that I could "get done" and dutifully report back to my new spiritual director. An addict to control, I like getting things *done.*

But my grief work went on for several hours. And then it stretched across that entire summer. In many ways, it continues still today.

My brother hanging me by my feet over the banister,
    laughing with his friend, and threatening to drop me
    on my head when I was a child.

My best friend Matt's fatal car crash on that terrible night
    when I was seventeen.

Sam's suicide.

The horrifying political massacre in Addis.

Being mugged by those three men on that dark street and
    then screaming in my sleep for years afterward.

Being rejected and neglected by my spiritual mentors.

Young Brother Eyob's fatal head wound.

The suffering of Ethiopia's street children like Precious
    and Eyob.

Ermi's brain cancer.

Mom's stroke.

My parents' mortality.

Twenty-six items ended up on my list of grief. Each one
broke over me with a thunderclap of tears.

That summer, I started doing grief work in earnest. I wrote
letters to myself and God about these wounding places of poverty. I
allowed myself to re-enter the house of these memories. To face the
fears hidden within them. To listen to the degrading voices hissing
through them. And to talk back to them. I re-remembered my
memories and practiced trusting that God was actually present with
me and holding me, even when I felt most anguished and alone.

One grief was particularly excruciating for me: facing Lily's
inevitable death off in an unknown future. Maybe later today?
Maybe tomorrow? Maybe in fifty years?

As I tried to write that letter to God, electricity surged
through my body and up my arms. I felt like I was going to
blackout and fall backwards in my chair. I wept hysterically,

hyperventilating with overwhelming distress. It was the closest I've ever come to feeling like I was about to die.

As Morrison saw, I had to "step through." I had to face my fear, enter into that shaking, flashing, hissing house haunted with trauma, and allow myself to grieve the death of Beloved. The unprocessed sadness inside of me wasn't evil in itself. But it wasn't going away on its own. And it had become so built-up and heavy that it felt like it was crushing my chest and cutting off my breath. The acute anxiety, pulsating pressure, aggressive voices, and impulse to harden myself by *doing more* were actually symptoms of *something else*: the unprocessed pain of my poverty.

When I started stepping through, I found suppressed traumas, neglected devastations, and unwept heartbreaks inside myself. They surged through my body and burst out of my eyes. I discovered that processing grief can feel like dying.

But it didn't kill me. To my surprise, it healed me.
Grief worked.

Jesus' Second Blessing

This is where Jesus leads us next on his Beatitudinal Way: *Blessed are the grieving, because they will be comforted.*

We're all poor. We all need to grieve. And we all need to be comforted.

No matter how "strong" and "resilient" we may imagine ourselves to be, we can't bypass the haunted house of mourning. This is an essential way-station in our journey of becoming humanely happy. And so, Jesus invites us into our grief and gives us permission to process what lives inside of us.

Like the poor, Jesus' blessing on the grieving was born out of his own experience. Likely in his late twenties, Jesus' best friend Lazarus got sick and died. When he died, like my best friend Matt died, Jesus didn't harden himself like I did. He stepped through. *Jesus wept.*

This is perhaps the profoundest sentence in the entire Bible: *Jesus wept.* He didn't "hold it together." He didn't offer cheap words of distraction. He also didn't apologize for his grief. He was so troubled inside and overwhelmed with emotion that he overflowed with tears (John 11:35).

Importantly, this wasn't a one-off "loss of control" either. It seems that Jesus wept frequently—by himself, with his friends, in public. He wept when Lazarus died. He wept over Jerusalem's addiction to violence when he entered the city for the final time before his execution. He wept convulsively in the face of his own panicked fear of dying. Some of his final words were a grief-stricken shriek of lamentation: "My God, my God, why have you forsaken me?"

Why did Jesus weep so frequently and freely?

We've seen that Jesus was a poor person born to poor parents in an animal shelter. He was nearly killed by the local politician and chased away as a refugee. He grew up under imperial occupation and witnessed executed bodies hanging from crosses. He never owned a home and lived in constant vulnerability. John, his spiritual hero, was beheaded for speaking truth to power. His beloved friends died of disease. Insults, character assassinations, and death threats hounded Jesus from the start of his movement.

Through all of this, Jesus intimately knew the damage and degradation of othering and empire. He was afflicted with loss. And so, Jesus went deep into his haunted house and spent significant time there. His tears flowed freely.

The difficult memories, the burning eyes, the pounding head, the spinning mind, the heaving chest, the sorrow-shattered heart, the shaking body riddled with disappointment—Jesus experienced all of this and allowed himself to be present to it. In this way, the philosopher Søren Kierkegaard said that Jesus made "a covenant of tears" with everyone who weeps.[8]

And so, Jesus blessed others with permission to grieve. When he was about to be executed, Jesus didn't tell the women watching this atrocity to toughen up or plead for his release. He urged them to *weep*. To feel just how terrible this atrocity truly was. To process their pain, lest it possess them.

Jesus' Beatitudinal Way meets us *here*—in our pain. He invites our fully embodied selves to be present in this place. His blessing is full of acknowledgement and promise: *Blessed are the grieving, because they will be comforted.*

The fact is, poverty is grievous. In whatever form it takes, it wounds us. It steals. It slashes and shakes. It disappoints and disappears. It hisses and withers. It leaves holes, casts shadows, mutes colors, and unravels threads. Poverty traumatizes us and tries to trap us in the past. It closes the future and strangles who we hope to become. It triggers tears, cried or uncried, and carves out vast hollows within us in which tidal waves of emotion flood, crash, and rage.

> Maybe it's the mother who died in childbirth.
> Or the bombing of your home.
> Or the promise that was broken.
> Or the soul-shattering separation.
> Or the numbers in your phone that you can no longer text or call.
> Or the event that ended the happiness you desperately hoped would never end.

In my experience, the heart of grief is loss. And maybe this

8 Søren Kierkegaard, *Eighteen Upbuilding Discourses*, ed. and trans. Howard V. Hong and Edna H. Hong (Princeton, NJ: Princeton University Press, 1990), 264.

52

is why grief is so frightening: loss touches our primal fear that we'll be abandoned and ultimately alone. That we'll lose Beloved.

Actively grieving our loss makes us feel even more vulnerable, to our own pain and the possibility of still more loss. After all, who likes being around grieving people?

So we tell ourselves to become hard, lest we lose everything. *Suck it up! Armor up! Get over it! Vulnerability is dangerous! Fake it til you make it!* Whatever our manic voices happen to hiss. "So we keep it all inside, and hide it deep in a drawer," sings the band Arcade Fire.[9]

But Jesus says that there's no need to suppress the painful reality of being poor humans. We don't need to pretend that we're something we're not. We don't need to perform that we're "more blessed" than anyone else.

The prosperity ideology sells this crack. It pushes us to shoot up an appearance of happiness defined as health, wealth, and winning as proof that we're really "blessed." Really "worthy" of being wanted. *Beloved.*

Divergent, Jesus blesses the *grieving.* It isn't shameful or unspiritual to acknowledge and express our heartbreak. We don't need to fight back our tears or apologize for being emotional. Authentic faith doesn't force us to harden ourselves and act as if we're invulnerable, unaffected, "on top." We can feel our feelings, deep down to the bottom. We can let that primal ocean of tears flow through our bodies and wash over our faces.

Blessed are the grieving, because they will be comforted. This is Jesus' promise to us.

The word for "comfort" that Jesus uses here— *paraklethesontai*—is important. It's used over a hundred times in the New Testament. Jesus named the Presence of God as our

9 Arcade Fire, "Age of Anxiety," track 1 on *We* (Columbia, 2022).

Paraclete or Advocate. It literally means that the grieving will never be abandoned by the One who is always by our side (*ad-*) and cries with us (*vocate*). Inspired by Jesus' teaching, the Harvard philosopher Alfred North Whitehead wrote, "God is the great companion—the fellow-sufferer who understands."[10]

Of course, our poverty and grief often make us feel like the exact opposite is true. Like we're alone with nothing left but loss, absence, and the dull struggle to survive. But Jesus promises us that God is there and always will be.

Those who are soaked in tears and shaking with sorrow are not shameful or left to themselves. They're safe to be softened. When it's all said and done—or unspeakable and undone—our vulnerability won't be shamed and exploited. Our hurt won't be humiliated. The grief-stricken have an Advocate.

They're blessed and destined for comfort.[11]

Crisis 2: Vengeance or Nonviolence?

This takes us to our second moment of decision, our second crisis, on Jesus' Beatitudinal Way: Will our grief enrage us and drive us toward grieving others? Or will our grief soften us and nourish nonviolent presence within us and between us?

Coming home to our haunted house can be enraging. Processing our inner pain requires doing dangerous work

---

10 Alfred North Whitehead, *Process and Reality*, second edition (New York, NY: Free Press, 1979), 351.

11 Jesus uses a word for grieving (*penthéō*) that typically refers to mourning for a loss. It's often paired with the word for weeping. After Jesus was killed, Mark tells us that Jesus' community was "grieving and weeping" (Mark 16:10). Jesus had become yet another loved one who was murdered by the empire, yet another absence in their punctured, impoverished world. And they did exactly what Jesus taught them to do: they grieved and wept.

We see an example of this grief and Jesus' promise of comfort in Paul's story (2 Corinthians 7). Paul was a religious extremist who persecuted followers of Jesus. But then Paul started following Jesus and experienced persecution himself. The blowback was grievous. Paul describes not being able to sleep, being harassed by religious violence, enduring conflict outside and fear inside, and being depressed. But then his friend Titus visited him and "comforted" him. A loving presence came to him in his pain, and he was advocated for or given "the courage to be" as Paul Tillich wrote.

with radioactive materials. It can stir up distressing memories of suffering, injustice, and victimhood. Deep shames, bitter resentments, and incendiary angers may surface and seize us.

We discover that ungrieved grief doesn't go away. It mutates and metastasizes. Unprocessed, it spreads and sickens. When it reaches the boiling point, our pain may bond us to others in pain. Eventually, it becomes explosive and drives us toward punishing whoever we happen to blame for our suffering.

The root of the word "punish" is *pain*. When we punish, we're often *painishing*. We're redistributing our pain in the desperate hope that inflicting it on others will make us feel better. Maybe less alone. More powerful. Vindicated. Soothed.

We easily seek a sick solidarity in our suffering by making others suffer. Of course, we all lose, but at least we're not alone. In the process, our coping mechanism reproduces the very things we seek to relieve: our poverty and grief.

Once more, Etty Hillesum understood the critical decision that faces us here. As she faced her own poverty and the "cosmic sadness" of the Holocaust, she discovered how essential it is for us to grieve our grief.

Not long before she was deported to Auschwitz, Etty wrote in her journal:

> "Your sorrow must become an integral part of yourself, part of your body and soul. You mustn't run away from it, but bear it like an adult. Do not relieve your feelings through hatred. Do not seek to be avenged on all German mothers. For they, too, sorrow at this very moment for their slain and murdered sons. Give your sorrow all the space and shelter in yourself that it's due, for if everyone bears their grief honestly and courageously, the sorrow that now fills the world will abate. But if you do not clear a decent shelter for

your sorrow, and instead reserve most of the space inside of you for hatred and thoughts of revenge—from which new sorrows will be born for others—then sorrow will never cease in this world and will multiply. But if you have given sorrow the space its gentle origins demand, then you may truly say: life is beautiful and so rich. So beautiful and so rich that it makes you want to believe in God."[12]

Etty's wisdom is precious but paradoxical. If we make space for our grief, we prevent it from overwhelming and controlling us. It slowly abates and integrates into who we're becoming. As Toni Morrison narrated in Beloved, our haunted house may even become a cherished home of deep connection and radical solidarity with others—even with people we once despised as "enemies."

Etty did this. She opened herself to the pain of others. Astonishingly, she even allowed herself to grieve with German mothers—those who gave birth to the soldiers who were destroying her world. In this divergent work, she confessed that she rediscovered beauty, richness, and God, even amidst genocide.

Beyond our wildest hopes, Beloved may return.

Like poverty, grief is the great unionizer of humanity. We all suffer it. No one escapes it. And if we allow ourselves to step through and enter into it—and then step even *further* into the grief of *others*—our painishing slowly converts into gentleness.[13]

Here the grievous cycle of our vengeance turns into a healing circle of solidarity. Real comfort and advocacy unlock and embrace us. Baldwin said it like this: "If I know that my soul trembles, and I know that yours does too; and, if I can respect

---

12 Hillesum, *An Interrupted Life*, 96-97.

13 Various forms of accountability and prevention of further harm may be necessary as we grieve together. We'll see this in Jesus' fourth way-station. He doesn't bypass justice. But this is very different from punishing/painishing as we'll also see.

this, both of us can live. Neither of us, truly, can live without the other."[14]

But the crisis of our choice is truly critical. If we suppress our grief, don't give it the space it needs, and refuse to tremble together, our pain pressurizes. It then easily boils over into a painishing flood of resentment, hatred, revenge, and violence. Sorrow multiplies.

Elisabeth Kübler-Ross captured Etty's insight in a single sentence: "Grief must be witnessed to be healed." Two thousand years before, Jesus understood this. When we grieve our grief and share presence with others in theirs, we are blessed. Comfort is promised, and a new union becomes possible.

This is the heart of Jesus' third blessing.

---

14 Baldwin, *Collected Essays*, 571.

CHAPTER 5

Way-Station 3: Nonviolence

*For Elias Chacour: Thank you
for teaching me God does not kill.*

"The way of violence leads to bitterness in the survivors and
brutality in the destroyers. But the way of nonviolence leads to
redemption and the creation of the beloved community."
Dr. Martin Luther King Jr.[1]

---

1 Martin Luther King Jr., "My Trip to the Land of Gandhi," in *A Testament of Hope: The Essential Writings and Speeches of Martin Luther King Jr.*, ed. James Washington (New York, NY: HarperOne, 1991), 25.

The Imitation Game

Long before the Ethiopian civil war exploded in 2020 and I started getting death threats, massive grief had been boiling for over a century. This grief was both intensely political and inescapably personal.

Late in the nineteenth century, Ethiopia's ruler Menelik II expanded the legendary empire through bloody conquests. Whole groups of people were dominated, humiliated, and displaced from their ancestral homelands. Poverty spread. Grief began boiling.

Then in 1974, Emperor Haile Selassie was violently overthrown by a military coup. The new communist dictatorship known as the Derg then unleashed a "Red Terror." Dissidents were disappeared. Mothers were forced to pay for the bullets that murdered their children. Hundreds of thousands of people were killed. Grief boiled hotter.

Then in 1991, a rebel movement called the TPLF overthrew the Derg. They established a new governing coalition called the EPRDF and promised to right these historic wrongs. Over the next 27 years, Prime Minister Meles and his "Revolutionary Democracy" made significant progress in recognizing the rights of all Ethiopians, developing the economy, and enshrining democratic freedom—on paper at least. The country boasted one of the fastest growing economies in the world. In the shadow of 9/11, itself an explosion of grief, the U.S. partnered with Ethiopia to wage its "War on Terror" in neighboring Somalia. Maybe you've seen *Black Hawk Down*.

But in reality the new regime increasingly ruled in the way of the old beaten path: crushing dissent, jailing opponents, killing with impunity, and establishing supremacy. I'll never forget hearing the rattle of machine guns in October 2005. I had just moved back to Ethiopia for the second time.

I soon discovered the source of that awful sound: the police had opened fire on protesters. Two hundred people were killed in the streets of Addis that day. In many ways, the body politic was literally and symbolically dismembered. More grief boiled and increasingly boiled over.

With time, massive protests turned into "Days of Rage" led by Jawar Mohammed, a young activist who later became my friend. Jawar channeled this rage in reaction to another government atrocity, this time at a cultural festival just outside Addis where Lily's dad lives.

By 2018, Ethiopia had become ungovernable. The crisis was so severe that Prime Minister Hailemariam did something almost unprecedented in Ethiopian history: He resigned.

In his place, a little-known spy chief in the EPRDF was appointed prime minister. He also happened to be a Pentecostal Christian.

Abiy Ahmed was quickly hailed as a messiah. Ominously, many called him Ethiopia's Moses. He himself designed his expensive new office suite in the shape of Noah's Ark.

In the flood of Ethiopia's increasing conflict, Abiy made many positive reforms and promised to usher Ethiopia into unprecedented "prosperity." In fact, he rebranded the old "Revolutionary Democracy" as the "Prosperity Party." His dream was to transform Ethiopia into the most powerful country on earth by 2050.

As my friend Tom Gardner, East Africa correspondent for *The Economist*, reported, Ethiopia became ecstatic with "Abiymania." It seems the wider world did too. In 2019, Ethiopia's "Pentecostal Putin" was awarded the Nobel Peace Prize.[2]

But the grief-turned-rage had never really been given the "space it was due," as Etty urged. Ethiopia never stepped through.

————

2 See Tom Gardner, *The Abiy Project: God, Power, and War in the New Ethiopia* (London: Hurst, 2024), 3.

According to the Ethiopian writer Rihana Nesrudin:

> "Ethiopians have a way of dealing with trauma by not dealing with it at all. We live both our personal and political lives as experts at evading and hiding away from harsh truths, never learning that the very emotions we attempt to bury—pain, hate, powerlessness—are those which come back at a later period in the ugliest of ways."[3]

I suspect Rihana is describing most of our cultures. The rapturous euphoria that clamored around Abiy was just the other side of the enraged grief that launched him to power. The former evaporated; the latter didn't go away.

When it served his power, then, in late 2020, Abiy weaponized this rage into the twenty-first century's deadliest conflict. Less than a year later, the Ethiopian historian Dr. Semeneh Ayalew wrote, "[Ethiopia] has become a large community of pain." This pained and painishing community produced "a dizzying daily multiplication of death and violence."[4]

What made Ethiopia's civil war so grievous wasn't only its dizzying destructiveness: around 1.2 million people killed, five million neighbors displaced, and twenty million bodies made to hunger. Its vicious cruelty shattered the soul.

During the war, I met privately with Abuna Mathias, leader of Ethiopia's fifty-million-member Orthodox Church. This elderly apostle spoke to me with grief in his soft voice. He said, "The eyes of our conscience have been blinded." Whole groups of people were dehumanized and called "cancers," "hyenas," and "devils"—

3 Rihana Nesrudin, "What Happened to Birtukan Mideksa?" *Addis Expressions*, August 25, 2024, addisexpressions.com.

4 Semeneh Ayelew, "Ethiopia: The Grim Search for Political Light in a Crisis," *The Elephant*, August 6, 2021, https://www.theelephant.info/analysis/2021/08/06/ethiopia-the-grim-search-for-political-light-in-a-crisis/.

including by Prime Minister Abiy. Viciously genocidal speeches were given by influential Christian leaders allied to Abiy. Their flocks responded with gleeful applause.

Ethiopia's new Noah/Moses had unleashed an apocalyptic flood of genocidal violence. Gruesome videos emerged of (likely Christian) soldiers burning (likely Christian) civilians alive. Tens, if not hundreds, of thousands of girls, women, and grandmothers were raped and mutilated, often in front of their families. Vital civilian infrastructure like schools, hospitals, and factories were systematically looted and destroyed. The region of Tigray—home to millions of Ethiopians—was blockaded, and countless people starved to death. After my friend (whose name I can't mention for his safety) returned from the region, he sounded shaken and distressed. He said that he'd never seen anything so terrible in his long career of doing disaster relief.

Even so, Abiy insisted upon his Zionist Ethiopian nationalism and prosperity gospel. He brazenly said that there was "no hunger in Ethiopia," even as millions were famished. He declared that homelessness had been "solved," even as the streets of cities were surging with displaced people. In fact, he boasted that the country was like an airplane on its ascendant runway to "prosperity."

Many of Ethiopia's most prominent Christian leaders rallied around their new Moses and defended his "just" war. They denied documented atrocities and tried to discredit anyone who called for a nonviolent solution. For over two years, the war remained wildly popular in mainstream Ethiopia.

Violence raged as a spasm of grief shook the country from corner to corner. The civil war killed around 1.2 million people or 1.5 times as many victims as the Rwandan genocide. Tom Gardner wrote that Christian leaders "arguably did most to publicly bless the war and sanctify its excesses."[5]

⸻

5 Gardner, *The Abiy Project*, 313.

Christians *blessed* genocide.

Ethiopia's civil war offers a sobering case study for all of us. It demonstrates what becomes possible when our grief isn't given the space it needs and our hearts becomes hardened.

As we've seen, ungrieved grief doesn't magically evaporate—whether in individuals, groups, or entire societies. It builds and boils and eventually explodes, as Langston Hughes wrote. What emerges can be shocking as rage radicalizes into vengeance and violence escalates into genocidal war crimes.

When we allow ourselves to look honestly in this mirror, the pattern of violence is an unmistakable dead end. In Ethiopia's uncivil war, one group attacked, killed, displaced, raped, and looted their "enemies." Then, power changed hands and the "other" group attacked, killed, displaced, raped, and looted their "enemies." Poverty upon poverty. Grief upon grief.

Of course, the warring parties ferociously condemned each other. With "God" on their side, they claimed to be nothing like each other: light and darkness, angels and demons, humans and hyenas. It seems we always do this.

But the irony was bitter and obvious: these literal enemy-siblings looked like mirror images of one another. They raged down the same violent path of vengeance. And what followed was death, displacement, and destruction.

This is what war always produces. With each denunciation of "the enemy" and every promise of "victory," the outcome was the same: more grinding poverty and more woeful grief. Except, that is, for the leaders at "the top" in Noah's Ark who called the shots and profited from the flood of bloodshed.

We shouldn't fool ourselves with false innocence: this pattern isn't unique to Ethiopia.

Wherever we find ourselves, violence has an uncanny capacity to reproduce itself as we imitate one another's rage. Yes, we furiously denounce one another. We might claim to be nothing like each other. But we still share a core belief that violence can keep us safe and forge a path to prosperity and power out of our poverty and grief.

So we mirror one another. Before our own poverty and grief are processed, we begin impoverishing and grieving others. We painish.

As this pattern raged in circles, I lost whatever faith I once had in "just war." I know this tradition intimately. At the University of Chicago, I was the last PhD student of the late Jean Bethke Elshtain, one of the world's leading scholars of just war theory and an adviser to President Bush after 9/11. Jean remains someone I deeply admire amidst our fierce disagreements.

But during the Ethiopian civil war, I became an atheist of the "God" of violence. I was compelled to abandon the belief that painishing others can help us overcome our pain. The words I had heard years before in occupied Palestine from Elias Chacour, a Christian elder who survived terrible Zionist violence mere miles from the place where Jesus taught the Beatitudinal Way, echoed back in my memory:

God does not kill.

Jesus' Third Blessing

Looking back quickly, Jesus promises us that the poor will fully belong in the kingdom of heaven and the grieving will be comforted. Jesus' third way-station is equally defiant and divergent. He declares for his traumatized, polarized audience and all of us to hear, *Blessed are the nonviolent, because they will inherit the earth.*

As we've seen, Jesus was intimately familiar with the wounding pattern of violence. He narrowly escaped a targeted massacre as a child. His cousin and spiritual inspiration, John, was beheaded by the local tyrant. The landscape of Jesus' life was crossed with gruesome executions. Death threats dogged Jesus from early on and never really stopped. His whole society was seething with enraged nationalist movements against the Roman Empire and yearning for a new Moses who would usher in prosperity.

How easy hardness, rage, and violence would have been for Jesus to justify. How easy to imitate and bless *this*. On the heels of slavery in Egypt, this is what Moses did for Israel, and we don't have any record of anyone objecting.[6]

But Jesus dared to step through. He grieved his grief and blessed another path. It looks something like this:

We're blessed if we've broken out of the repetitive pattern of trying to overcome poverty and grief by impoverishing and grieving others. We're blessed if we've allowed ourselves to be softened by suffering and let tears wash through our pain. We're blessed if we're able to cry with others but refuse to make others cry.

As we traverse this first stretch of the Beatitudinal Way, we've lost the desire for more suffering and sorrow for anyone else. Othering appalls us. Supremacy sickens us. We've started sobering up from wanting to be above anyone else. We no longer aspire to be "on top" and "more blessed" than others. Trusting this pattern to solve our problems strikes us as an insane addiction, like shooting up the same old crack and expecting something new. We've allowed our poverty and grief to sober and soften us into a nonviolent presence.

The word Jesus uses for nonviolence in his third way-station can also be translated as "meek" or "gentle" (*praei*). It suggests regulated strength and harnessed power free of violence.[7]

Jesus uses this word to describe himself in relationship

---

6 It wasn't until centuries later that the Hebrew prophets spoke of God's blessing on Israel's "enemy" neighbors. Like all prophets do, they regrounded their community's vision in God's original promise of blessing for all people. See Isaiah 19:23-25 and Genesis 12:1-3.

7 Note that in 1 Timothy 3:3, "gentleness" (ἐπιεικῆ) is used as the opposite of "violence." See Walter Wink, *Jesus and Nonviolence: A Third Way* (Minneapolis, MN: Fortress Press), 2003.

with people who are vulnerable, exhausted, and overwhelmed. He says, "Come to me, all you who are weary and burdened, and I will give you rest. Take my pattern upon you and learn from me, because I am *gentle*" (Matthew 10:28-29).

Jesus uses this word again to describe his path when he enters Jerusalem for the last time before his execution. Riding on a donkey rather than a war horse, Jesus weeps over Jerusalem's addiction to violence and declares that he is *nonviolent* (Matthew 21:5). From start to finish, Jesus presents himself as a meek human, a gentle presence who can be trusted to resist exploiting others' vulnerability and longings for vengeance.

Jesus made this powerful gentleness the epicenter of his message. After introducing the Beatitudinal Way, he taught something that was unprecedented but fully aligned with his nonviolent path of becoming humanely happy. He declared, "Love your enemies" (Matthew 5:43).

For Jesus, this decision to love even the most hateful was about breaking out of the imitation game by imitating God. Jesus believed that God is creative and powerful. He said, "God is kind to the ungrateful and wicked" (Luke 6:35). In fact, Jesus described God's gentle goodness as the very core of God's divinity (Matthew 5:45; Luke 6:36).

From this perspective, practicing enemy-love and nonviolent resistance in the face of oppression isn't foolish or weak. It's courageous. In fact, it conspires with the most elemental, innovative way of our divine Parent. It's *divine*. Gandhi called it "the supreme virtue of the brave."[8]

Jesus gave several examples of what he had in mind when he blessed nonviolent practice. Each demands a more grounded power. This power is characterized by *responsive creativity*

---

8 Gandhi, *On Nonviolence*, 50.

rather than *reactive conformity*. It's an agile agency unshackled from rigidity that unlocks the spiral of violence. It flows from the softening work of grief and the expanded range of movement that it opens up.

Here are a few examples that Jesus gave to illustrate how to practice nonviolence.

First, if a soldier forces you to carry their pack one mile, as Roman imperial law dictated, voluntarily walk with them a second mile. Assert your agency. Demonstrate that you're not a dehumanized doormat to be used and discarded. Project your personhood with defiant presence. Exert the freedom to make your own choices. Confront humiliation with a display of your own dignity and a confounding act of togetherness.

Second, if someone slaps you on your right cheek, turn toward them with your left cheek. Stand your ground. Face the violent. Unmask the weakness of their aggression with your own compassionate countenance. Refuse to cower or be conformed to their belittling behavior. Like the face of God, shine with peace in the face of violence.

Third, if someone curses you—cheapens you, insults you, reduces you to something small—don't let them dictate the script of your response. Rewrite their othering box with a blessing. Speak dignity to them. Name your desire for them to be well. Defy damnation with words of hope. Revoice what language is for with the grammar of God who speaks blessing to all people from the very beginning.

Fourth, if someone tries to take your coat, give them the shirt off your back. Expose their greed with your own generous flesh. Let the skin on your beloved body expose and shame the extractive, ugly rag of domination. Whatever you do, refuse to put the straightjacket of supremacy on your own precious frame.

And through it all, forgive. Assert your freedom by unhostaging others. Don't let them inject the crippling poison of bitterness into your system. Deflect their hook into the addictive cycle of violence. As Audre Lorde wrote, "The master's tools will never dismantle the master's house."[9] Be free like God and open a new future rather than replaying the past. Hold on to people and let go of their painishing.

Jesus actively practiced this creative nonviolence to the end of his own life. Like Gandhi, Jesus understood that, "Without a direct active expression of it, nonviolence is meaningless."[10] As Jesus *practiced* nonviolence, he promised that people who convert their poverty and grief into this gentleness will inherit the earth.

Admittedly, it might not seem so now. The nonviolent harbor the very rational fear of endlessly being displaced and dominated by the violent. After all, people who practice nonviolence are often labeled as weak. We know the cynical, dismissive script of violence by heart: "unrealistic, "idealistic," "utopian." The nonviolent may even be targeted as *traitors* as we'll see in Jesus' eighth way-station.

Jesus certainly was. If we practice his path, we may feel unearthed and alienated from the current order of things. The (dis)order of violence is heavily invested with much faith, money, energy, storytelling, identity, glory, spite, and spectacle, just like it was in the Roman Empire that executed Jesus.

But the gentle will have a home, Jesus fearlessly promises. In fact, when God's new creativity is finally welcomed, the whole earth will belong to the nonviolent. They are prophets of God's dream, embodiments of our planetary future. If you want to see where the world is going, Jesus says, don't follow the beaten path of vengeance's dead-end. Look to the nonviolent.

They show us how everything starts over in the end.

---

9 Audre Lorde, *The Master's Tools Will Never Dismantle the Master's House* (London: Penguin UK, 2018). I'm grateful to my friend Natalie Avalos for pointing me to Lorde's text.

10 Gandhi, *On Nonviolence*, 50.

Does Nonviolence Actually Work?

As I said, we know the script of violence by heart. It's in our bones. But if you're thinking that Jesus' nonviolence sounds good on paper but is idealistic and ineffective in the real world, it actually isn't.

Harvard Professor Erica Chenoweth has researched the effectiveness of violent versus nonviolent methods for bringing sustainable change in conflict-ridden societies. Her study stretched from 1900 to 2019. Between these 120 years, she examined 627 cases. This is a massive data set.

Chenoweth set out to debunk nonviolence. But analyzing the data, Chenoweth discovered that nonviolent civil resistance is *twice as effective* as violent methods for bringing sustainable change. It's *always* successful when just 3.5 percent of a society's population commits to a nonviolent campaign. Nonviolence works *every time* when people get *organized*. Unexpectedly, Chenoweth ended up debunking violence.

Much more could and should be said here. But, in short, the nonviolence that Jesus innovated isn't idealistic and ineffective. It's actually realistic and effective. Dr. King's mentor Howard Thurman was right: "Christianity as it was born in the mind of this Jewish teacher and thinker appears as a technique of survival for the oppressed."[11]

When we look at the data, nonviolence hasn't been tried and found wanting. It's been unwanted and left untried, including by most Christians after Constantine came to power.

The keys are the courageous conviction to diverge from the old, ineffective-but-orthodox beaten path of violence and the collective organizing that makes something new possible. As Gandhi declared, "There is no such thing as defeat in nonviolence.

---

11 Thurman, *Jesus and the Disinherited*, 18-19.

It is the only true force in life."[12]

This is Jesus' prophetic promise: sooner or later, the nonviolent *will* inherit the earth—and make it habitable for the rest of us. Like poverty and grief, nonviolence is the great unionizer of humanity. When we take it seriously, nonviolence ultimately *works*.

How to Become Invincible

Yet again, Etty Hillesum is a potent witness of Jesus' promise and what our best social science increasingly proves.

As we've seen, Etty suffered extreme poverty and excruciating grief under Hitler's hardened, genocidal pedagogy. Her journals are raw with pain. But Etty meditated on Jesus' words "day and night" and walked his way into the most astonishingly powerful nonviolence.

As she faced deportation to the death camp, Etty named what she considered to be truly "essential" in life. This is how she described it:

> "Between our eyes and hands and mouths there now flows a
> constant stream of tenderness, a stream in which all petty
> desires seem to have been extinguished. All that matters
> now is to be kind to each other with all the goodness that
> is in us."[13]

As her world was darkened with violence, Etty entered into a new lucidity. The petty desires of othering were no longer attractive to her. Tenderness, kindness, goodness are all that matter and the essence of being humanely happy.

But Etty's kindness was no fuzzy sentimentalism. It was a fierce embodiment of courageous faith and creative agency.

---

12 Gandhi, *On Nonviolence*, 50

13 Hillesum, 164.

In 1942, Etty was forced to register as a Jew at the Gestapo office in Amsterdam. This was essentially her death sentence. That same day, she wrote about the cruel treatment that she suffered from the Nazi officer there. But Etty wasn't crushed or conformed. She journaled:

> "The rottenness of others is in us, too. I see no other solution, I really see no other solution than to turn inward and root out all the rottenness there. I no longer believe that we can change anything until we have first changed ourselves. And that seems to me the only lesson to be learned from this war."[14]

The Nazi officer who registered Etty into Hitler's genocidal system represented the "final solution" that would kill Etty, kill her family, and kill six million of her people. But Etty chose self-examination rather than condemnation. She saw that this nonviolent response is truly the final solution to violence.

And so, she resisted the easier imitation game of rage and refused to submit to vengeance. Rather than mirroring the othering that attacked her existence, she faced herself and confessed, "no human being is alien to me any longer... I can find the way to people of every sort."[15] We witness that Etty's grief work *worked*.

In this way, Etty processed her pain and chose her path: "despite all the suffering and injustice, I cannot hate others."[16] Having examined herself and renounced hatred, her vision cleared even further. She described learning to see every person "as a dwelling dedicated to You, oh God."[17]

---

14 Hillesum, *An Interrupted Life*, 84.

15 Hillesum, *An Interrupted Life*, 99.

16 Hillesum, *An Interrupted Life*, 86.

17 Hillesum, *An Interrupted Life*, 205.

Astonishingly, as Etty reflected on her life soon before being sent to Auschwitz, she reported being "strangely *happy*."[18] What buoyed her spirit wasn't a change in her situation or an expectation of miraculous deliverance. It was a change in *herself*, in who *she* was becoming. Her hardy-but-unhardened heart was maturing into what she called "a new gentleness"[19]—even amidst genocide. This growth in *gentleness* is what made her strangely *happy*.

Etty had become a radically nonviolent presence in the face of some of the cruelest, most catastrophic violence in history. She wasn't naive. She admitted that "those who hate have good reason to do so." But she continued her self-examination and made her choice in the fiery space between on the Beatitudinal Way:

> "Why should we always have to choose the cheapest and easiest way? It has been brought home forcibly to me here [in the camp] how every atom of hatred added to the world makes it an even more inhospitable place. And I also believe, childishly perhaps but stubbornly, that the earth will become more habitable again only through the love that the Jew Paul described."[20]

Etty chose the nonviolent creativity that Jesus pioneered. This is the radical power that transformed Paul from being a religious nationalist and murderous terrorist into the author of the timeless words "Love never fails" (1 Corinthians 13).

Having given herself to this way of becoming humanely happy, Etty wrote a few more astonishing words at the very end of her life:

---

18 Hillesum, *An Interrupted Life*, 165.

19 Hillesum, *An Interrupted Life*, 165

20 Hillesum, *An Interrupted Life*, 256.

"Essentially, no one can do me any harm at all. Yes, children, that's how it is: I am in a strange state of mournful contentment."[21]

Etty was *blessed*. She had become *invincible* in a *Nazi camp* that would send her to her death. She faced her poverty. She stepped through into her grief. She matured into a fiercely gentle nonviolence. And this is where it took her: *Essentially, no one can do me any harm at all!*

This is the humane happiness we all long for. As I reflect on Etty's life and her "strange state of mournful contentment," Jesus' promise to the nonviolent unfurls in my imagination with vivid realism.

If we're sober, who else but the gentle could inherit the earth? Who else but the meek could welcome the rest of us home without turning it back into a death camp? Who else but the nonviolent would have the audacious imagination and creative character to embark with God on something so truly daring and *divergent*—a new earth, a restarted history, a healed humanity?

Etty's "new gentleness" wasn't weak or unrealistic. It heralded God's future. She rooted out her own "rottenness" and rejected hatred for anyone with nonviolent love as her final solution.

This is how the imitation game ends. This is how "the earth will become more habitable again," as our best social science now demonstrates.

And so, divergent, Jesus declares, then and now, *Blessed are the nonviolent, because they will inherit the earth.*

When we suffer poverty, step through it into grief, and God's kindness converts us to nonviolence, we come home to a new world and show everyone else the way there. We don't need

---

21 Hillesum, *An Interrupted Life*, 288.

to fear being dominated and displaced. We have become harmless and unharmable—even in crucifixion and genocide.

Dr. King distilled this wisdom to its most basic clarity and potent power. He declared, "The way of violence leads to bitterness in the survivors and brutality in the destroyers. But the way of nonviolence leads to redemption and the creation of the beloved community."[22]

Crisis 3: Withdrawal or Justice?

Etty, King, and Jesus are incredibly inspiring, no doubt. But they're equally haunting.

When we move through our grief into gentleness, we become even more vulnerable than we already were. Nonviolence isn't a way of life armored with threats of death and ammoed up with weapons of mass destruction.

As we'll see at the end, Jesus' Beatitudinal Way is risky. No wonder so few chose this path in Germany's Holocaust and the genocidal violence of Ethiopia's civil war.

This sobering fact takes us to our third moment of decision, our third crisis, on Jesus' Beatitudinal Way: Will our practice of nonviolence wither into withdrawal from the world? Will we wait for a magic fix off in a nebulous future? Or will our nonviolence churn inside of us and convert into a hunger and thirst for *justice*?

Etty powerfully described her "turn inward" and decision to root out the rottenness within herself. But we can easily stop here and passively resign ourselves to the brokenness of our world.

Will we disengage into inaction? Or will we open ourselves to the burning ache for things to be made right, here and now?

This is the heart of Jesus' fourth blessing.

————

22 King, *A Testament of Hope*, 25.

CHAPTER 6

Way-Station 4: Justice

For Roger and Greg: Thank you for not checking out.

"Never forget that justice is what love looks like in public."[1]
Cornel West

---

1 Cornel West has made this statement many times in numerous places.

The Ache

Working up an appetite for justice can come with an agonizing hunger. It may even feel like starving to death.

The body of our existence craves for the solid nourishment of real change. We want to see results, here and now.

But so often, a dull emptiness is all that we find in the pit of our stomach. All too quickly, our soul invisibly eats away at itself. We thirst for healed relationships, but the well seems dry. Our being becomes parched. Our head pounds with pain. Our shocked system feels like it's turning against itself.

After Lily and I transitioned into exile from Addis to Chicago, the chair of Wheaton College's political science department, Professor Michael McKoy, invited me to teach "Introduction to Peace and Conflict." I was honored but didn't think I could do it. Like the BitterSweet Retreat, I planned to (im)politely decline.

The topic felt too close to home. This was 2023, after all—my year of poverty, grief, and aggressive self-doubt. A kind friend meant to encourage me when he said, "You could teach that class in your sleep!" But his words made me feel even more intimidated. The truth is, I didn't feel like I had anything to teach anyone. *Nothing.* I was sorely tempted to withdraw.

But Lily and my board at the Institute for Faith and Flourishing comforted me. And so, I ended up saying yes.

Unsurprisingly, I designed the course with a focus on Ethiopia's civil war, the deadliest conflict in the twenty-first century. Leading scholars and practitioners generously agreed to speak with my students. Each session was powerful. But I'll never forget our night with Selam, who joined us along with experts from the World Peace Institute and Harvard Law School.

Selam is a Tigrayan educator and anti-war activist. She has extensive experience and a disarmingly kind presence. She's led major public demonstrations against the war and given interviews on many of the world's largest media platforms.

At the start of our session, I asked Selam to share her experience and help us understand the real consequences of the war in Ethiopian society. The survey of injustice that Selam set on the table was soul-sickening. As she spoke, the ache in the classroom grew deeper and heavier.

Selam told us about soldiers massacring civilians. Even people who sought sanctuary in historic churches were slaughtered. She estimated that 800,000 persons had been killed in the violence. (The current estimate is around 1.2 million casualties.)

Selam's research further indicated that tens, if not hundreds, of thousands of girls and women had been raped. Many had foreign objects inserted into their bodies to humiliate and torture them. Family members were often forced to watch or even participate in this cruelty.

Moreover, schools, hospitals, and businesses were ransacked and destroyed. In the wreckage, a whole generation was growing up impoverished, illiterate, and sick. A famine reminiscent of the hellish nightmare of Ethiopia's 1984 "Great Famine" haunted the region. Selam told us, "An entire generation is highly traumatized." I would only add "traumatized *again*."

But then, Selam began to speak about her own personal experience of the war. She said, "Our advocacy to stop the conflict has cost us massively. My father was hunted and held in captivity." The air drained from the room. We listened in suspense.

Selam described receiving a phone call from an unknown number late into the night. The man on the other side of the line said, "If you don't stop what you're doing, I'll kill him."

Selam told us, "I had to make the very difficult choice: Do I remain silent, or keep fighting and ensure the sacrifice of my father doesn't go in vain?"

Selam didn't finish her gutwrenching story. Ever focused on others, she pivoted back to telling us about the suffering of women in Tigray.

But when she paused for questions, I awkwardly asked, "Selam, how is your dad now? Is he safe?"

My father is not safe. They killed him.

I've taught for many years in many different contexts around the world. But I don't remember a classroom ever feeling quite like that. We were exhausted, utterly empty, aching in our bowels for things to be *better*.

Selam was given an impossible choice. She could withdraw into passive silence and maybe save her dad's life—even as millions of her people continued suffering. Or she could continue raising awareness about the war and advocating for justice—and likely spend the rest of her life without her dad.

Selam told us, "I had to choose the latter. These are the sacrifices we make."

This is the ache of those who hunger and thirst for justice. Selam's experience may be more severe than yours or mine. But I suspect we've all felt the shooting spasm of pain in the bowels of our being for things to be *better*. To be different. To be less broken and terrible.

Jesus' Fourth Blessing

Glancing back again, Jesus has blessed the poor, the grieving, and the nonviolent. He now takes us another step forward on the Beatitudinal Way. To his polarized and war-torn audience and to all of us today, Jesus declares, *Blessed are those who hunger and thirst for justice, because they will be filled.*

As Selam's story painfully illustrates, it'd be far easier and safer to withdraw, to fall silent and surrender to injustice. The current (dis)order of things can seem impervious and unchangeable. Many of us sit back and passively wish for a magic fix in another world.

But Jesus' pacificity isn't passivity. The core petition of his spirituality is for God's justice to *"come on earth* as it is in heaven"—*not* our escape to another world. And so, Jesus blesses people like Selam who dare to ache and sacrifice for justice, here and now. Against so many appearances, he promises that they will be *filled*.

Justice means different things to different people. It's a crucial but controversial concept. Popular culture often equates justice with punishment and retribution. This is the old imperial maxim of *quid pro quo*: "this for that." Give what you get.

What did justice mean to Jesus?

Thankfully, we don't need to guess. Jesus spelled out his vision of justice immediately after he introduced the Beatitudinal Way. In many respects, the Sermon on the Mount is Jesus' justice manifesto. It serves as the foundational message of his entire movement (Matthew 5-7).

The heart of justice for Jesus is *right relationships of mutual flourishing*. This is why Jesus repeatedly focuses on the quality of our relationships as he unpacks what he calls "practicing justice" (Matthew 5:19-20; 6:1, 33). Gandhi described it as "a way of transforming relationships so as to bring about a peaceful transfer of power, effected freely and without compulsion by all concerned, because all have come to recognize it as right."[2]

In other words, justice is what happens when God, people, and creation are loved, respected, and cooperate with trust. Jesus captured it like this: "In everything, do to others what you want them to do to you. This sums up the Law and the Prophets" (Matthew 7:12). More simply, *Love your neighbor as yourself*, as

2 Gandhi, *On Nonviolence*, 35.

the whole Bible teaches at its best.[3]

James Baldwin stated this in reverse: "It is a terrible, an inexorable, law that one cannot deny the humanity of another without diminishing one's own: in the face of one's victim, one sees oneself."[4]

In his divergent Sermon on the Mount, then, Jesus speaks to five primary dimensions of justice, just like Moses gave his five books of Torah. Let me briefly unpack Jesus' Torah of justice.

First, justice radically respects human dignity (Matthew 5:21-26).

As a baseline, it prohibits killing other people. But it reaches much deeper. Justice uproots the othering mindsets and insulting words that make degrading people and committing violence possible to begin with.

Contemporary social science has conclusively demonstrated that mass conflict and war always begin with *othering*.[5] The war of weapons starts with the war of words. By this, I mean the things we say that represent others as unrelated or less than ourselves. Unsurprisingly, then, Jesus fiercely repudiates insults and anger. He knows that degrading others is the gateway to "the fire of hell" (Matthew 5:22).

In short, real justice is emotionally grounded. It recognizes

---

3   See Leviticus 19:13-19, 33-34; Matthew 5:43-48; 19:18-21; 22:37-40; Mark 12:28-34; Luke 10:25-37; John 13:34-35; Romans 13:9-10; Galatians 5:13-15; Ephesians 5:1-2, 25; James 2:1-13; 1 John 4:19-21. For a comprehensive study, see my book *Neighbor-Love: How an Ancient Revolution Can Overcome Othering and Heal Our World* (Downers Grove, IL: IVP Academic, 2025).

4   Baldwin, *Collected Essays*, 179.

5   Crucial studies on "othering" or how we come to see others as unrelated or less than ourselves include Toni Morrison, *The Origin of Others* (Cambridge, MA: Harvard University Press, 2017); Sam Keen, *Faces of the Enemy: Reflections of the Hostile Imagination* (New York, NY: Harper & Row, 1986); David Livingstone Smith, *Less Than Human: Why We Demean, Enslave, and Exterminate Others* (New York, NY: St. Martin's Press, 2011); and john powell and Stephen Menendian, *Belonging Without Othering: How We Save Ourselves and the World* (Stanford, CA: Stanford University Press, 2024). My forthcoming book explores othering in detail: *Reviving the Golden Rule: How the Ancient Ethic of Neighbor-Love Can Heal the World* (Downers Grove, IL: IVP Academic, 2025).

the precious value of "others" and respects them as our *neighbors*.

Second, justice actively seeks to resolve and transform conflict. It refuses to play the imitation game.

We see that Jesus so highly values human life and the quality of our relationships that he elevates human reconciliation above divine worship. He says that if you're at your place of worship but have unresolved conflict with others, you should interrupt your worship and "first go and be reconciled" (Matthew 5:24).

In other words, worship that disregards human worth is unjust and empty religion (Matthew 6:14-15). This teaching sounds less sentimental when we remember that the vast majority of the violence in the American founding, German Holocaust, Rwandan genocide, and Ethiopian civil war was committed by people who went to church and identified as Christians.

We saw in the previous chapter that Jesus mobilized his vision of justice with the practice of nonviolence (Matthew 5:38-48). The heart of this practice is creative, courageous agency that confronts injustice without *conforming* to it. Nonviolence defies evil but holds the door open to transformation and healing.

Once again, the heart of justice for Jesus is neighbor-love or recognizing and respecting the precious value of others (Mathew 7:12; 22:39). As such, authentic justice strives to repair old relationships or to create new ones, even with our enemy-neighbors.

Baldwin said it like this to his Black nephew in the face of American white supremacy: "The really terrible thing, old buddy, is that you must accept them. And I mean that very seriously. You must accept them and accept them with love."[6]

Third, justice faithfully embodies integrity and builds trust.

---

6 Baldwin, *Collected Essays*, 293.

In the context of the family, this integrity begins by honoring covenant relationships and uprooting the egocentric ways that we betray and exploit one another. Justice purifies how we see others with our eyes and touch one another with our hands. It protects and nourishes the sacred bonds between our bodies. In this way, it nurtures self-esteem, stability, and security (Matthew 5:27-32).

More broadly, justice tells the truth and keeps promises. In fact, Jesus says that swearing oaths becomes redundant in the practice of justice. This is because truthfulness is so fundamental to justice. Divergent to culture, Jesus teaches, "All you need to say is simply 'Yes' or 'No'" (Matthew 5:37).

What's at stake here is *trust* or social capital. When our words and actions match, trust thickens between people. With trust, we can rely on one another, and creative cooperation becomes possible. Through cooperation, we can do far more together than we could ever do on our own.

Innovation and mutual flourishing are the nourishing harvest of justice.

Fourth, justice overcomes economic inequity by renouncing greed and practicing generosity (Matthew 6:1-4, 19-24).

If the heart of justice is love and respect for the dignity of others, passively accepting inequality and the suffering of others violates justice. Here we see again that Jesus' vision of economic justice flows out of his theology: "God is kind to the ungrateful and wicked." Our Parent is a generous Giver of gifts as elemental and essential as sunshine and rain, regardless of who we are and whether we deserve them.

Unsurprisingly, then, Jesus teaches that the way we engage with others experiencing injustices like social humiliation, food insecurity, homelessness, lack of medical care, and unjust imprisonment is crucial to how God will judge us when our earthly journey ends. In fact, he says that how we treat *these others* is how we actually treat *God* (Matthew 25:31-46).

In short, authentic justice isn't only *restorative* in the face of conflict. It's also *redistributive* in the face of inequity. Family values without social justice fall short of right relationships of mutual flourishing. Our house remains haunted with evil.

Finally, an honest, trusting, humanizing relationship with God is essential to justice according to Jesus (Matthew 6:5-34).

Moments after laying out the Beatitudinal Way, Jesus introduces the one and only prayer that he ever taught, the Lord's Prayer or Our Father. I've written a whole book about it and warmly invite you to explore *Flourishing on the Edge of Faith: Seven Practices for a New We*.

Strikingly, Jesus only taught this prayer *after* teaching the other four dimensions of justice. What's clear is that he believed an intimate relationship with God orients and energizes our relationships with others. But Jesus was serious when he said that religion that disregards human relationships is woefully wrong.

And so, Jesus starts with the horizontal human-to-human dimensions of justice and only then moves to the vertical human-to-divine dimension. Jesus sees these as inseparable carats in the diamond of justice.

There's plenty more that Jesus said about justice. But this is the heart of it. It's what Jesus surely had in mind when he declared, "Blessed are the hungry and thirsty for justice."

We're blessed when we crave for human dignity, nonviolent conflict transformation, trustworthy integrity, redistributive equity, and spiritual vitality. This is the Torah of *humane* happiness.

The Way of Justice

Jesus didn't peddle abstract principles. His teaching was rooted in real life, and he loved concrete examples. His teaching on justice is no exception. Jesus pointed to his fiery cousin John and called his work "the way of justice" (Matthew 21:32).

John distilled his "way" into the word *metanoia*, usually translated as "repentance." We typically think of this as individualistic introspection and a cosmic beatdown. But it meant something wildly, refreshingly different to John.

For him, *metanoia* meant reimagining God's desire for humanity and reorienting our entire lives around it. James Baldwin captured John's spirited vision like this: "God is, after all, not anybody's toy. To be with God is really to be involved with some enormous, overwhelming desire, and joy, and power which you cannot control, which controls you."[7]

John pinpointed three dimensions of God's desire that map the way of real justice (Matthew 3:1-12; Luke 3:2-14). They distill Jesus' vision. Let me briefly survey them. The first dimension of justice is human equality.

John declared that people who elevate their identity above others should abandon this Zionist, supremacist mindset. In this way, he boldly rejected religious nationalism with its idea that some people are "more blessed" than others and destined for special "favor" from God. In fact, John targeted this sense of superiority as a primary barrier to a right relationship with God and others (see Matthew 3:7-10; Luke 3:7-9).

With his prophetic snark, John said that people can trace their identity all the way back to Abraham himself, the founding parent of faith itself. But if this Abrahamic identity leads us to believe that we're better than anyone else, it's just dust.[8]

_____

7 Baldwin, *Collected Essays*, 220. I'm grateful to Pastor Michael Rudzena of Good Shepherd New York for the phrase "cosmic beatdown."

8 Peter was Jesus' closest student, and yet he still held on to a supremacist mindset for years. He wouldn't enter the homes of others that he saw as dirty because they weren't part of his group. After he had a major experience of *metanoia*, he said, "I now realize how true it is that God does not show favoritism but accepts from every nation the one who honors God and practices justice" (Acts 10:34-35).

Real justice recognizes the worth of all people and embraces this face-to-face standing. It's what Dr. King called "a person-to-person perspective" instead of a "master-servant perspective."[9]

Human equality obviously locks into the primacy of human dignity in Jesus' vision of justice. The second dimension of justice is economic equity.

John said that people with extra wealth should share it with others in need. John specifically highlighted the importance of clothing, food, and shelter (Luke 3:11). God's desire is for all of us to have our basic needs met.

When we hunger for justice, the purpose of abundance is generosity and interdependence—not private accumulation and inequality. As Paul, the former religious nationalist, wrote, "Your plenty will supply what others need, so that in turn their plenty will supply what you need. The goal is equality" (2 Corinthians 8:14).

Economic equity locks into Jesus' redistributive vision of justice. The third dimension of justice is responsible power.

John said that people with power should refuse to abuse it (Luke 3:12-14). Power is a responsibility to serve, not a right to dominate. Real justice is not an insider's game; it's equal justice for all.

Responsible power clearly locks into Jesus' vision of integrity, nonviolence, and praying for God's kingdom to come on earth, here and now, as it is in heaven.

Rethink identity, redistribute wealth, and restrain power: this was John's *metanoia*. It's what Jesus called "the way of justice."

All throughout, right relationships of mutual flourishing are the heart of it. Today we call this conflict transformation, peace building, and restorative justice.

9 Martin Luther King Jr., "Playboy Interview," in *A Testament of Hope: The Essential Writings and Speeches of Martin Luther King Jr.*, ed. James Washington (New York, NY: HarperOne, 1991), 359.

As we've seen, John was a bold nonconformist and public reformer. He didn't accept the religious nationalism, economic inequality, and power politics so pervasive in our relationships, then and now. He dared to critique corruption and violence at the highest levels of authority.

And John paid the price for it. In his early thirties, he was imprisoned. Not long after, he was beheaded by Herod Antipas, the son of Herod "the Great." This was the ruling establishment that tried to kill Jesus as a child.

Notice, then, that Jesus was being extremely audacious when he called John the greatest prophet in history and pointed to *his* work as the *way of justice*. Jesus openly identified with a public enemy on death row who was about to be executed.

Apparently, Jesus thought the risky guilt-by-association was worth it. This is how highly Jesus valued justice. He celebrated John as justice's most compelling champion.

In light of John's prophetic life and painful death, Jesus' fourth blessing is even more defiant: *Blessed* are the *hungry* and *thirsty* for *justice*.

If you're starving for human equality; if you crave for everyone's needs to be met; if you burn for the end of oppressive political power—divine desire is churning inside of you. Your humanity is longing for what it was made for, a nourishment as elemental as food and water.

And with equal defiance, Jesus promises that the justice-starved will be *filled*.

This is the same word the Gospels used when Jesus multiplied a meal for 5,000 hungry people. In that feast, everyone was "satisfied." There was so much food that everyone ate what they wanted, and there was plenty leftover for later.

Fullness is the state when all needs are met and our longing is brought to complete contentment. Jesus promises that if we're aching for right relationships of mutual flourishing now, we'll be fully satisfied in the end. An everlasting feast of justice is already being set before us. Reality has a reservation at this abundant table. God is not on a diet.

Right now, hungering for justice can feel terrifying. It may strike us as unappetizing and even nauseating to desire. Isn't justice just a bitter recipe for starvation?

Selam's words rattle in my heart: *My father is not safe. They killed him.*

But Jesus tells us not to fear allowing this elemental hunger and thirst to churn inside of us. We won't starve. Burn for justice. Desire it, despite everything.

Fullness is our cosmic destiny.

Crisis 4: Condemnation or Compassion?

We now arrive at our fourth moment of decision, our fourth *crisis*, on Jesus' Beatitudinal Way: Will our craving for justice stunt into condemning others? Or will it expand into compassion for all who suffer and ache for mercy?

Like the churning of an empty stomach and the pounding headache that comes with dehydration, our desire for justice is divinely designed. It's an alarm of life enfleshed in our souls that tells us something essential is urgently needed. Othering attitudes and oppressive systems *should* sound this alarm and trigger our hunger and thirst. We were made for better. John, Salem, and others have risked their lives to remind us that we were made for justice.

But our craving for justice can quickly kill compassion. If we're not careful, our ache for *right* relationships replaces *real* relationships altogether. Instead of being-with and being-for one another in our impoverished, grief-stricken fallibility, we easily assume the posture of the judge "at the top" *above* one another. We begin evaluating everyone on our scale of perfection and failure. We then mark people for approval or condemnation. As the saying goes, justice becomes "just us."

At some point, our fixing project to reform the world runs out of fuel. We start damning one another. Discarding one another. Displacing and destroying one another. We discover that injustice is its own ruinous punishment, a screwdriver that vandalizes the soul and societies alike.

Of course, we continue calling this *devastation* "justice." We might even call it *God's* justice. The beloved Hebrews did after they escaped 400 years of being ground down by Egyptian slavery.

But before we know it, we're playing the imitation game again. The soul-sickening cruelty that Selam described in Ethiopia's civil war spirals out of control.

"Justice" withers into loveless retribution and punishment. It recycles the endless pattern of *painishing* one another. We find ourselves shackled to a bloody table that never satisfies us or makes things right. Hunger for healed relationship mutates into gleeful pleasure in others' pain.

More poverty and grief are the poisoned fruit. As Baldwin observed, "The suffering of the scapegoat has resulted in seas of blood, and yet not one sinner has been saved, or changed, by this despairing ritual."[10]

Jesus never lost touch with the heart of real justice: right relationships of mutual flourishing.

And so, the conclusion of his justice manifesto is brilliantly anticlimactic. It isn't a crusading commission to go out, judge others, and condemn all that doesn't conform. It's a blunt warning against this painishing impulse: "Don't judge, or you too will be judged... *Treat others the way you want to be treated*" (Matthew 7:1-5, 12, 24-27).

---

10 Baldwin, *Collected Essays*, 386.

The philosopher Cornel West captures the essence of Jesus' justice in a single sentence: "Never forget that justice is what love looks like in public." If it isn't, justice has lost its way.

This is the heart of Jesus' fifth blessing.

CHAPTER 7

Way-Station 5: Compassion

*For Tekalign: Thank you
for your endless compassion.*

"The killer in me is the killer in you."[1]
The Smashing Pumpkins

1   The Smashing Pumpkins, "Disarm," track 6 on *Siamese Dream* (Virgin Records, 1993).

A Balm for All Wounds

Even as we survey Ethiopia's civil war, it's difficult to imagine injustice more atrocious than the Holocaust. The scale of violence was soul-shattering. Six million Jews, gays, and other minorities were systematically murdered. The quality of cruelty was sickening.

Hitler's "hard pedagogy" was disastrously effective. His followers became just as "violent, domineering, undismayed, and cruel" as he promised. Precious human lives were treated as worthless animals. People were hunted, packed into cattle cars, worked to death, and then slaughtered.

Right relationships were ripped apart in every way imaginable. Poverty, grief, and violence exploded.

And yet, in the face of this radical evil, two of the Holocaust's most courageous victims followed Jesus' divergent pedagogy into a more radical compassion: Etty Hillesum and Dietrich Bonhoeffer.

Both ached for justice. Both struggled for right relationships of mutual flourishing. But both refused to become condemning and punishing in the process. Somehow, they became even more self-aware, empathetic, and merciful.

They practiced compassion even toward the perpetrators of this catastrophe.

Etty chose compassion on February 25, 1942. It was the day her life began to end.

As we've seen, Etty was forced to register her Jewish identity at the Nazi police station in Amsterdam. This was essentially her death sentence. Jews were being registered so they could be rounded up, sent to "work" camps, and then murdered en masse. Etty knew this.

Predictably, the Nazi officer at the station that day treated Etty as less than human. He was domineering and hardened by

Hitler's supremacist pedagogy.

In the face of this injustice, Etty had every reason to condemn this man as the epitome of evil—to do to him what he was doing to her. *Quid pro quo.* He represented the genocidal system that was literally creating hell on earth for Etty and her entire community. (Jesus wasn't exaggerating when he warned that othering unleashes "the fire of hell.")

But Etty didn't respond by condemning this man—or anyone else for that matter. She had exited the imitation game and resisted mirroring his injustice. Instead, she responded with compassion.

First, Etty looked inward and examined her own capacity for evil. At this time, her friend Jan had asked her with outrage, "What is it in human beings that makes them want to destroy others?" Etty's response was striking:

> "Human beings, you say, but remember that you're one yourself. The rottenness of others is in us, too. I really see no solution than to turn inward and root out all the rottenness in there. I no longer believe we can change anything in the world until we have first changed ourselves. And that seems to me the only lesson to be learned from this war."[2]

Etty had surrendered the illusion of moral superiority. She was willing to face the "rottenness" in herself. She saw herself as a full participant in the human struggle, including the powerful desire to destroy others. And so, she refused to other the others othering her.

Second, Etty chose empathy. She sought to understand this young Nazi officer. She asked herself what experiences of suffering he himself may have had. She wondered if he carried traumas and disappointments that manifested in his cruelty. She

---

2 Hillesum, *An Interrupted Life,* 84.

also interrogated the unjust systems that had dominated and deformed him, *systems* like Hitler's "hard pedagogy."

Instead of seeing this Nazi officer as inherently evil—as an enemy or subhuman monster—Etty saw him as a hurting, fallible *person*. His untransformed pain had trapped him and was now being painishingly transferred to others.

Third, Etty chose to stop that painishing cycle with mercy. She wrote in her journal:

> "I know that I am dealing with human beings and that I must try hard to understand everything that anyone does. And that was the real import of this morning: not that a disgruntled young Gestapo officer yelled at me, but that I felt no indignation, rather a real compassion, and would have liked to ask, 'Did you have a very unhappy childhood, has your girlfriend let you down?' Yes, he looked harassed and driven, sullen and weak. I should have liked to start treating him there and then...

> What needs eradicating is the evil in man, not man himself... Do not relieve your feelings through hatred, do not seek to be avenged on all German mothers. For they, too, sorrow at this very moment for their slain and murdered sons."[3]

Etty's hunger for justice stretched into compassion rather than strangling it. She refused to generalize, curse, or condemn. Instead, she examined her own "rottenness." Then, she sought to understand the painful poverty and insecure grief hidden behind the cruelty of others. And, again and again, she chose compassion—even for the Nazis and their mothers.

Astonishingly, the last words in her journal read, "We

---

3 Hillesum, *An Interrupted Life*, 86, 97.

should be willing to act as a balm for all wounds."[4]

Despite Everything

Etty wasn't alone in her compassionate response to Nazi genocide. Her life and writings remind me of Dietrich Bonhoeffer (1906-1945).

Bonhoeffer was a brilliant German professor of theology who finished his PhD when he was twenty-one. He was also a loving pastor and courageous anti-Nazi dissident. Robert Coles called Bonhoeffer one of the top-ten moral leaders of the 20th century. I've had the privilege of sitting at his writing desk twice in Berlin.

In 1933, Hitler came to power. Days later, at the young age of twenty-six, Bonhoeffer became the first Christian leader to speak publicly against the dangers of Hitler and Nazism. Thereafter, he devoted his career to training dissident Christian leaders to follow the Beatitudinal Way of Jesus against Nazified, genocidal Christianity. He helped Jews escape from Germany and traveled throughout Europe to sound the alarm about the horrific atrocities of Hitler's regime.

But as Bonhoeffer hungered and thirsted for justice, his own life was emaciated.

In 1936, he was banned from teaching at the University of Berlin.

A year later, his underground school for anti-Nazi pastors was shut down by the Gestapo. Many of his students were arrested and sent to the frontlines as eighty-nine percent of Christian leaders swore loyalty to Hitler in Bonhoeffer's home region of Germany.[5]

---

4 Hillesum, *An Interrupted Life*, 231.

5 See Eberhard Bethge, *Dietrich Bonhoeffer: A Biography*, revised edition (Minneapolis, MN: Fortress Press, 2000), 601.

In 1940 and 1941, Bonhoeffer was banned from public speaking and publishing his prophetic writings. To his eternal honor, the Nazi authorities judged that he lacked "the requisite political reliability" because Bonhoeffer had engaged in "activity subverting the people."[6]

A year later, Bonhoeffer was expecting to be arrested or killed. He wrote a will and gave it to his best friend Eberhard.

Then on April 5, 1943, the Nazis finally showed up at his parents' home where he lived in the attic. They promptly arrested him and took him to prison.

A few months earlier on Christmas Eve, Bonhoeffer had given his family and friends an essay entitled "After Ten Years." This essay was his meditation on a decade of living under Hitler's supremacist dictatorship.

During this time, Bonhoeffer had witnessed his society, his Christian community, and his colleagues and friends descend into some of the most appalling othering and hellish injustice in history. His brother Walter had been killed years before in the First World War. Now in the Second, Bonhoeffer himself lost many of his most beloved rights, freedoms, and friends to totalitarian terror.

What did Bonhoeffer say after ten years of this injustice? He wrote:

> "Nothing of what we despise in another is itself foreign to us. How often do we expect more of the other than what we ourselves are willing to accomplish? Why is it that we have hitherto thought with so little sobriety about the temptability and frailty of human beings? We must learn to regard human beings less in terms of what they do and neglect to do and more in terms of what they suffer. The

6 See Dietrich Bonhoeffer, *Conspiracy and Imprisonment: 1940-1945: Dietrich Bonhoeffer Works, Volume 16*, ed. Mark Brocker (Minneapolis, MN: Fortress Press, 2006), 182.

only fruitful relation to human beings—particularly to the weak among them—is love, that is, the will to enter into and to keep community with them. God did not hold human beings in contempt but became human for their sake."[7]

Bonhoeffer's response was uncannily like Etty's.

First, he chose to look inward and examine himself. He humbly acknowledged his own capacity to commit all the despicable deeds he saw being done by others in his society.

Second, Bonhoeffer refused to dehumanize the dehumanizers. He chose to see people empathically through the lens of their fallibility and suffering rather than their successes and failures. Hurt people hurt people. More simply, people *people*.

Third, Bonhoeffer kept love at the center of his ache for justice. In this way, he resiliently resisted succumbing to contempt. The will to enter into and keep relationship with others was his compassionate compass.

The next year would severely test Bonhoeffer's compassion. In the Tegel military prison, he survived what he called "repugnant" interrogations.[8] With each day, it was becoming increasingly clear that he wouldn't escape alive.

In the midst of this anguish, Bonhoeffer wrote another private meditation on July 7, 1944. What would he say this time?

If anything, his compassion had only become even more elemental and all-encompassing. Out of his poverty, grief, nonviolence, and ache for justice, Bonhoeffer wrote:

> "The just suffer from injustice, from the meaninglessness and perversion of world events... This is the chief hallmark

---

7 Dietrich Bonhoeffer, "After Ten Years," in *Letters and Papers from Prison: Dietrich Bonhoeffer Works, Volume 8*, ed. John de Gruchy (Minneapolis, MN: Fortress Press, 2010), 45.

8 Bonhoeffer, *Letters and Papers from Prison*, 606.

by which the just can be recognized, that they suffer in this way. To some extent they bring into the world God's own way of perceiving things; that is why they suffer just as God suffers at the hands of the world...

[But] that was God's response to the world that nailed Christ to the cross: blessing. God does not repay evil for evil, and thus the just should not do so either. No judgment, no abuse, but blessing.

The world would have no hope if this were not the case. The world lives by the blessing of God and of the just and thus has a future. Blessing means laying one's hand on something and saying: Despite everything, you belong to God.

This is what we do with the world that inflicts such suffering on us. We do not abandon it; we do not repudiate, despise, or condemn it. Instead we call it back to God, we give it hope, we lay our hand on it and say: may God's blessing come upon you, may God renew you. Be blessed, world created by God, you who belong to your Creator and Redeemer."[9]

It's difficult to believe that these beautiful words were penned in a Nazi prison cell. Bonhoeffer intimately knew the traumatizing "meaninglessness and perversion" that the Nazis had mass-produced at industrial scale. He had suffered grievously. But as his suffering churned into his soul, his compassion went deeper still.

And so, this was his posture to the end: no judgment, no

---

9   Dietrich Bonhoeffer, "Daily Text Meditation for June 7 and 8, 1944," in *Conspiracy and Imprisonment: 1940-1945: Dietrich Bonhoeffer Works, Volume 16*, ed. Mark Brocker (Minneapolis, MN: Fortress Press, 2006), 632 (translation modified).

abandonment, no condemnation. *Blessing*. Even in Nazi Germany.

Bonhoeffer reached out his hand and put it on a world that was murdering millions of his Jewish neighbors, murdering his students, murdering his family and friends, murdering he himself. And he declared, "Despite everything, you belong to God."

This radical compassion is what he called "God's way of perceiving things."

Jesus' Fifth Blessing

As Etty and Bonhoeffer walked Jesus' divergent path, they went deep into his fifth way-station. To them and to us still today, Jesus declares, *Blessed are the compassionate, because they will be mirrored with compassion.*

By this point on Jesus' Beatitudinal Way, we're intimately familiar with human finitude, fallibility, and failure. We know the pain of poverty, our smallness and suffering. We've stepped through into the haunted house of our grief. We've started feeling at home in the vulnerability of nonviolence. We're working up a fierce hunger and thirst for justice.

In all of this, we've started processing our impulses toward hardness, vengeance, withdrawal, and painishment. We've begun facing the fact that we're broken creatures who suffer. We make painful mistakes. We get things badly wrong. We harm one another in both microscopic and catastrophic ways.

Perhaps we've started to see what Baldwin saw: "None of us are that different from one another, neither that much better nor that much worse."[10] People *people*. As The Smashing Pumpkins sing, "The killer in me is the killer in you."[11]

---

10 Baldwin, *Collected Essays*, 747.

11 The Smashing Pumpkins, "Disarm," track 6 on *Siamese Dream* (Virgin Records, 1993).

On the rugged terrain of this painful path, Jesus says that we're blessed if we travel onward into compassion.

At heart, compassion is the willingness to be present with others in pain. As the political scientist Daniel Philpott writes, "it's the desire for others to be well and relieved of their suffering."[12] Compassion finds no glee in others' grief. It defies what Baldwin called "our disrespect for the pain of others."[13]

In this way, compassion is an embodied practice of self-aware generosity. Like we've seen with Etty and Bonhoeffer, it looks inward with honesty at our own rotten capacity to do harm. It looks outward with empathy at the suffering and insecurity hidden behind the harm that others cause. And it chooses to be a merciful presence in this pain rather than painishing those who painish us.

In his famous Parable of the Good Samaritan, Jesus gives us a picture of compassion. He says it looks like the practical choice to see others in their suffering. It then moves close to them, embraces them in their vulnerability, and does what it can to relieve their pain. He teaches, "Do this, and you will flourish" (Luke 10:37-38).

For Jesus, authentic justice matures into this practice of compassion for our mutual flourishing, or it simply isn't *just*.

And Jesus promises that the compassionate are truly *blessed*. They too will be mirrored with compassion.

Of course, the opposite often seems inevitable. It's a terribly frightening prospect. The compassionate open their souls and make room for the pain of others, even their enemy-siblings. But in response, they're often left to bear their pain alone or stabbed in the back. Like nonviolence in the face of grief, compassion in

12 Daniel Philpott, *Just and Unjust Peace: An Ethic of Political Reconciliation* (New York, NY: Oxford University Press, 2012), 63.

13 Baldwin, *Collected Essays*, 173.

the face of injustice is extremely vulnerable.

As I mentioned in my opening letter, people in your group may see your compassion for "others" as an unforgivable betrayal. For them, mercy is a telltale sign that you're secretly one of the "others" who must be eliminated.

At the same time, people on the "other side" may see your compassion as a weakness to exploit or a hidden agenda to attack. It's double jeopardy. Etty and Bonhoeffer experienced both.

In short, then, compassion may feel like a nobody's land of abandonment and attack. When justice has been reduced to painishment, compassion is easily criminalized. As I said from the start, those who love the enemy often *become* the enemy.

But Jesus fearlessly promises us that a merciful presence will meet us in our pain. We will not be abandoned or attacked forever. God's own unbreakable compassion will mirror us in the end.

It's a beautiful image: compassion endlessly mirroring compassion, back and forth in an ever-deepening bond of mutual care. The imitation game of vengeful injustice will ultimately be reverse engineered. It isn't our destiny. The mirror of mercy is where reality is finally revealed and set free forever.

Sacred Disobedience

Once more, Jesus' fifth way-station was an act of prophetic defiance, a sacred civil disobedience in the face of religious nationalism.

When Israel escaped from the genocidal injustice of Egyptian slavery, Moses blessed his people and criminalized compassion. He said, "You will be more blessed than any other people... You must destroy all the peoples the Lord your God gives over to you. Do not look on them with compassion" (Deuteronomy 7:14-16).

Sadly, the blessed ache for justice ended up vomiting up pain and justifying genocide. The eyes of compassion were told to look away from others in pain.

No wonder Jesus' practice of compassion gave him such a notorious reputation.

One day, a Canaanite woman approached Jesus and pleaded with him, "Have compassion on me!" Her child was sick, and she was desperate for help (Matthew 15:22).

But she was a Canaanite. And she was asking for the exact thing that Moses explicitly said Canaanites should never be given: compassion. In fact, Moses said that she *and* her *child* should be *killed*—not cured!

But Jesus was divergent.

After this woman took the risk of asking for his compassion, Jesus surrendered Moses' supremacist mindset. He chose mercy. He not only refused to follow Moses' genocidal order, he defiantly reversed it.

Jesus healed her suffering child. But then he went further. He *praised* this othered woman—a Canaanite!—for her *faith* (Matthew 15:28).

When we read the Gospels, we see that Jesus practiced compassion with all the wrong people. Roman soldiers who were occupying his homeland. Jewish tax collectors who colluded with the enemy. Zealots who wanted to overthrow them both. Jesus even developed relationships with members of the religious leadership that he so fiercely critiqued. He moved toward all the others he was expected to hate.

For Jesus, compassion wasn't a compromise of faith. It was the core of faith. He loved to quote the prophet Hosea who said, "I desire compassion not sacrifice" (Hosea 6:6). In Hosea's context, God was challenging Israel to choose loving others rather than "sacrificing" them for their religious identity.

Jesus used this verse in the same way. When the religious leaders complained that Jesus was identifying with sinners and disregarding the ultimate practice of Torah, Jesus cleverly quoted *God* in his defense: "I desire compassion not sacrifice" (Matthew 9:13; 12:8).

For me, the way Jesus died is the most compelling embodiment of his compassion.

For the previous three years, Jesus had opened his soul, crossed boundaries, and shared compassionate presence with seemingly everyone. He was a magnet of pain and a presence of compassion.

But Jesus wasn't mirrored. He was mocked and murdered.

By mainstream standards of "justice," then and now, Jesus' killers deserved to be damned. They should have been cursed to hell and abandoned to eternal torment.

Jesus could have done this. He could have condemned them and commissioned his followers to take revenge—an on-demand delivery of this hellish "justice" here on earth. Few, if any, would have objected.

But as he was crucified, Jesus stretched his soul open wider still. In this most painful moment of his life, he prayed, "Father, forgive them, because they don't know what they're doing" (Luke 23:34).

This was Jesus' way of saying with Bonhoeffer, "Despite everything, you belong to God." It was his way of becoming what Etty called "a balm for all wounds."

How did Jesus do this? It certainly wasn't automatic.

Like Etty and Bonhoeffer, Jesus self-examined. He processed his own poverty, grief, and capacity for violence. As he traversed the way-stations of his own path, he understood what his killers couldn't.

They were acting out of their own pain. They were conformed and carried away by culture. They didn't actually *understand* what they were doing. They *thought* that they were doing something significant: serving "God," defending their "nation," bringing a criminal to "justice." But they were recycling the trauma of their own unjust suffering and further entrenching the old beaten path. *Painishing*.

Jesus refused to imitate this pattern, because he trusted in another mirror. Through the eyes of God, he could see that even his killers still belonged. And Jesus wanted *them* to be *well*. Like Bonhoeffer after him, he entered into and kept community—even with these *others*.

And so, Jesus declares, "Blessed are the compassionate, because they will be *mirrored* with compassion." When we ache for justice and choose to expand into compassion rather than condemnation, we take another step in becoming humanely happy.

Compassion is the magic mirror of reality. It reveals what's really going on, whether we want to see it or not.

Crisis 5: Cynicism or Cleansing?

This brings us to our fifth moment of decision, our fifth crisis, on Jesus' Beatitudinal Way: Will our compassion collapse into cynicism? Or will it open us to see God?

The truth is tragic: compassion can be blinding. Compassion calls us to open our soul deeper and wider to pain—the pain of others, our own pain, the pain of all creation. At some point, it becomes hard to see anything else.

Look at Jesus, Etty, and Bonhoeffer. They embodied the exquisite beauty of compassion. But they didn't get mirrored.

They got mutilated.

Maybe you've chosen compassion and felt the soul vandalism as you were misunderstood, abandoned, or abused. This is the moment when we most need compassion ourselves. But we don't always get it. We give but don't get. Beloved dead again.

Opening the eyes of the soul with compassion is wildly risky. It can feel like getting stabbed with a screwdriver in our most intimate place of vulnerability.

Cynicism easily closes in. It mutters, "There's nothing more to see here. It's all the same: poverty, pain, and people ruining what's truly precious. Over and over again! Are you crazy? Stop looking."

The irony is brutal: the more we perceive, the darker the world can appear. The more we care, the cheaper life may seemingly become.

Compassion can be a scary, mucking business. When Selam described the injustice savaging Ethiopia and the murder of her own dad, holding the soul open with compassion one second longer felt excruciating, like starving to death.

I suspect all of us in the room that night were tempted to explode with condemnation. Or simply close off with a cynical shrug. Look how hopelessly terrible we humans appear to be.

The questions become acute and urgent:

Is God even there?

Is goodness real?

Do people actually matter?

Why keep the aperture of the soul open to being stabbed one. more. f*cking—time?

This is the heart of Jesus' sixth blessing.

CHAPTER 8

Way-Station 6: Cleanheartedness

For Dave: Thank you
for helping me see God.

"The idea that some lives matter less
is the root of all that's wrong with the world."[1]
Dr. Paul Farmer

---

1 Tracy Kidder, *Mountains Beyond Mountains: The Quest of Dr. Paul Farmer, a Man Who Would Cure the World* (New York, NY: Random House, 2009), 294.

The Dark Night of the Soul

Mother Teresa endures as one of the most famous champions of compassion in history. And rightly so.

Flawed though she was, she devoted her life to being a merciful presence with and for people in pain. Her love embraced abandoned street children, lepers whose bodies were rotting away, dying people whose low-caste status made them worthless in the eyes of their society.

Mother Teresa inverted Moses' mountaintop blessing and saw the filthy "tail" at the bottom as the beloved image of God.

Still, fewer people know that Mother Teresa's compassion nearly blinded her to God and goodness. For decades, she made private confessions to spiritual leaders in her life. But these confessions were kept strictly secret for years after her death.

When they were finally released, what was revealed wasn't a glorious light. It was a gouging darkness.

Here's just one example of what Calcutta's saint of compassion confessed:

> "The darkness is so dark—and I am alone.—Unwanted, forsaken.—The loneliness of the heart that wants love is unbearable.—Where is my Faith?—even deep, down right in, there is nothing, but emptiness & darkness—My God—how painful is this unknown pain. It pains me without ceasing.—I have no Faith—I dare not utter the words & thoughts that crowd in my heart—& make me suffer untold agony."[2]

Anguishing existential torment.

---

2 Mother Teresa, *Mother Teresa: Come Be My Light: The Private Writings of the "Saint of Calcutta,"* ed. Brian Kolodiejchuk (New York, NY: Doubleday, 2007), 186.

Mother Teresa's experience of spiritual darkness, extreme loneliness, and loss of faith went well beyond cynicism. Her crisis of compassion took her to the very brink of nihilism. The philosopher Friedrich Nietzsche potently described nihilism as the condition in which "'why?' finds no answer."

But the bittersweet truth is that Teresa wasn't alone. Countless people who have chosen compassion—including Etty, Bonhoeffer, and Jesus himself—have also had similar experiences of nihilistic despair.

The 16th-century Spanish mystic John of the Cross called this "the dark night of the soul." At the heart of this darkness is "the fear of being lost on the road, thinking that all spiritual blessing is over and that God has abandoned you since you find no help or pleasure in good things." It's the time when we fear "all good is gone."[3]

What a brutal irony: deep into Jesus' Beatitudinal Way, the beauty of compassion born from our ache for justice can lead us into spiritual blackout.

Jesus' Sixth Blessing

As we enter into his sixth way-station, we see afresh that Jesus has beheld the human psyche and our embodied experience with rare and sensitive perception. His Beatitudinal Way traces the labyrinth of the human condition.

But Jesus doesn't give us a cold, clinical diagnosis. He guides us onward with a fresh fire of blessing at the crucial bends where we so easily lose our way or fall off the cliff.

To his soul-vandalized audience then and to each of us in the dark night of our souls today, Jesus declares, *Blessed are the cleanhearted, because they will see God.*

---

3 John of the Cross, *Dark Night of the Soul* (Mineola, NY: Dover Publications, 2003), 25, 68.

At this seemingly God-forsaken juncture on our journey, it may seem like the lights have gone out. Like all good is gone. Bewildered in the darkness. Hopelessly lost.

We may even be tempted to regret our compassion as a foolish mistake to begin with. Why open our soul so wide to misery, only for it to be slashed and blighted and left to us useless?

With Mother Teresa, I've certainly doubted that God is still there—or ever really was.

In this intimately painful place, Jesus suggests that a mysterious *purification* is taking place through this mortifying process. It's what James Baldwin called, "the cleansing breaking of the heart which precedes atonement."[4]

A beautiful erosion is underway even as things seem to be falling apart. Here the bedrock of reality is slowly exposed.

For the first time, Jesus speaks directly of *God*. Here he promises something unprecedented in his religion. In fact, Jesus diverges from Moses once more and promises something that Moses had strictly *forbidden*: we will *see God*.

Moses explicitly taught, "No one may see God and live."

He tethered seeing God with mortal terror and certain death. When Moses stumbled into a visionary encounter with God, he "hid his face, because he was afraid to see God." Ironically, Moses imagined seeing God like seeing Pharaoh, the genocidal dictator who told him, "The day you see my face you will die!" (Exodus 10:28).

Out of his own fear, Moses forbade his people from even *desiring* this ocular intimacy with the divine. If they caught a glimpse of God, Moses warned that God would "break out" and *kill* them. God's unveiled presence was imagined as a savage,

---

4 Baldwin, *Collected Essays*, 839.

ruinous force (Exodus 33:20; 24:11; 19:22).

But Jesus defied Moses' teaching and deterrorized seeing God. It's not only that humans can somehow *see* God and *survive*. Jesus promised that seeing God is a *blessing* that God *desires* us to experience on the blindside of compassion. It's the key to our *happiness*.

Paradoxically, this new divine vision may emerge in the spiritual blackout when "that which is most clear and true is to us most dark and doubtful."[5]

Come Clean

A clean or pure heart is the secret to this theo-optics according to Jesus. But what he meant is very different from what we often associate with "purity."

Puritanism.

Holier-than-thou.

Judgmental separation from real human experience.

Refreshingly, real purity is the exact opposite according to Jesus.

Jesus spoke incessantly of the heart. He always associated it with the center of our selves, the core of our loves and desires. The heart is the nucleus of how we see and hear, our inner eye and inner ear. It's who we really are when superficial appearances are stripped away (Matthew 6:21; 13:15; 22:22-23; Luke 6:45; 12:34; 24:32).

And Jesus associated a *clean* heart with radical *humility*. The Celtic mystic John Philip Newell writes, "[Humility is] learning to live from the sacred common ground of life rather than lifting ourselves up over one another or separating ourselves from one another."[6]

---

5 John of the Cross, *Dark Night of the Soul*, 85.

6 John Philip Newell, *Sacred Earth, Sacred Soul: Celtic Wisdom for Reawakening to What Our Souls Know and Healing the World* (New York, NY: HarperOne, 2021), 187.

When our sense of superiority and separation is washed away, the clean heart is opened to see God in amazing ways. Even if we're not able to perceive this at first.

We see this pattern in Jesus' own rite of passage as he prepared to launch his public movement.

Jesus went down to the river Jordan to be baptized by John. As we've seen, John's way of justice was blunt and challenging. He called people to abandon thinking of themselves as better than anyone else because of their religion, ethnicity, wealth, or power. With this sense of superiority rinsed away, John told his listeners to share their resources generously and to resist using their power to exploit others.

To embody this embrace of *metanoia*—this revolutionized mind—John invited people to come out to the wilderness. Notice that this was far away from the Jerusalem Temple and its powerful establishment. There, on the edge of faith, John began dunking people in the Jordan River. This water ritual symbolized being liberated from the enslaving patterns of evil.

Sadly, baptism has become yet another marker of "superior" identity in some Christian circles long after John popularized it for the exact opposite purpose. But what it originally represented remains profound.

When you're baptized, you fall backwards into someone else's arms. You surrender control and allow yourself to be held by power outside of your own.

Then, your flesh becomes parallel with the earth. Your face points straight to the sky. You're no longer standing above anyone else. You embody the posture of death.

Finally, after your body is buried in water, you rise like a newborn baby emerging from the womb.

In this way, baptism is a radical ritual of new beginning. The grime of the old beaten path—encrusted in pride, profit, and power—is washed away.

John's baptism was obviously intended for "sinners." What I mean is that it was offered to people who realized they were at a dead-end in their lives and needed to start over.

Strikingly, Jesus joined them. He got in line. Waded into the water. And asked John to bury him in the river with everyone else.

It's one of the most provocative moments in the life of Jesus. John himself was confused and protested. He didn't think Jesus *needed* baptism. Jesus was *already* clean.

John was so embarrassed by Jesus' presence in the river that he told Jesus to switch positions and baptize *him*. But Jesus insisted.

And this was his paradoxical purity.

Ironically, abandoning the appearance of purity can be the surest proof of actually being pure. Jesus wanted to be soaked in solidarity with "others," especially the washed-up people who were publicly admitting that they needed to rethink their lives and start over in God's love.

Quite profoundly, then, Jesus chose to begin his movement with radical compassion. He told John that doing this "fulfilled all *justice*." It embodied the heart of right relationships of mutual flourishing: surrendering any residue of superiority to others and humbly seeking God's desire for humanity with others—*not* "above" them (Matthew 3:15).

John finally consented. He plunged Jesus under the river. Jesus fell backwards and was buried in water.

As his face pointed skyward and the river raced over his body, Jesus had a vision of God. Strikingly, this is the only time that the Bible records Jesus actually *seeing God*. Apparently, this singular vision captured everything he needed to behold.

As the water washes over him, Jesus sees reality open. The veil between transcendence and immanence, heaven and earth, suddenly vanishes. It all flows into one.

God's Presence then appears and gently descends onto Jesus' body. Jesus sees this Presence in the form of a dove.

Jesus' happiness in this moment is impossible to overestimate. The dove was an ancient biblical symbol of peace. It represented the entire earth being cleansed of all violence and born anew (Genesis 6:11; 8:10-11). Jesus sees "the God in whom their is no violence."[7]

With this sacred Presence hovering on his body, Jesus hears the words we all long to hear: *You are my beloved child; I delight in you*. With these words, our Parent announces to Jesus his core identity. God declares God's unconditional happiness with *who Jesus is*—a humble child of God embracing solidarity with other children of God (Matthew 3:17; Mark 1:11).

Recall Moses' warning: "No one may see God and live."

But Jesus not only sees God and lives. He sees God and comes *fully alive*!

What Jesus sees is nothing short of revolutionary in the history of religion. His divine vision overturns the archaic way we often imagine God and reality itself.

When the heart of the universe opens, God doesn't "break out" with terrorizing violence like a savage black hole. The opposite happens. A dove of peace appears out of the void. And a voice of Love reverberates from heaven with unconditional delight.

This is what we can all see and hear in the cleansing river of humble solidarity with others (1 John 3:1).

---

7 This beautiful expression comes from my friend Joel Aguilar Ramirez's book *A Human Catechism: A Journey from Violence and Collective Woundedness to Peacebuilding* (Eugene, OR: Wipf & Stock, 2024).

No doubt, this mystical experience of seeing God inspired Jesus to design the Beatitudinal Way the way he did. It begins with his strange declaration, "Blessed are the *poor* in spirit, because *theirs* is the kingdom of *heaven*."

I imagine Jesus simultaneously weeping and laughing as he remembered his baptism and crafted these sacred words. Jesus saw that eternal love opens everywhere for everyone. The gate of heaven is found where we least expect it: when we enter into the muddy river with the most devalued and discarded people on earth like Precious and her family.

When we glimpse through the veil and see what heaven holds, all fear is washed away. It's everlasting belovedness and belonging. *Beatitude.*

In this river, competition is cleansed. Happiness, wholeness, humanity belong to every one of us. Even us poor folk will be perfectly precious in the end. The kingdom of heaven embraces all who walk this divergent way of becoming humanely happy.

Jesus' baptism and sixth blessing reveal afresh how incredibly bold Jesus was. He defied Moses' dictum. He identified with sinners. And he promised that seeing God is possible for all whose hearts are washed in the waters of humility.

As we look at Jesus' life, we behold that humanity becomes clean paradoxically: by becoming unclean. By abandoning the mindset of being "purer" or "more blessed" than anyone else. The inspiring humanitarian doctor Paul Farmer called this supremacist mindset "the root of all that's wrong with the world."

When this gets swept away in the river, humble solidarity opens heaven. We're given the eyes to see God.

If there's any doubt that this is what Jesus meant by getting cleanhearted, he made it crystal clear with this provocative statement: "When it comes to the inner life, give to the poor, and you'll be totally clean" (Luke 11:40-41).

Jesus said this to religious elites who prided themselves on their superior status and used this privilege to enrich themselves. Jesus brilliantly turned this toxic purity culture inside out and taught that we're "totally clean" when we literally give up this mindset. Every time we renounce superiority and embody our equal preciousness by sharing our resources, it's like a micro-baptism in the river of God's love. The taint of being on top is purified.

Similarly, Jesus' brother James described "clean religion" as active faith that embodies compassion for the most marginalized and vulnerable people. This faith resists systems governed by privileging some and demeaning others.

In fact, James echoes Jesus' Beatitudinal Way as he unpacks his vision of clean religion and critiques its perversion: "God has chosen those who are poor in the eyes of the world to be rich in faith and to inherit the kingdom he promised to those who love him. But you have dishonored the poor" (James 1:27; 2:1-13).

Similarly, Jesus' student Peter associated purity with practicing "sincere love for each other, loving one another deeply, from the heart" (1 Peter 1:22).

If we've made it this far, we observe that what started in the beginning has really started to *sink in* now. We're all poor in spirit. We're all grieving. We all need gentleness and justice. Compassion has intimately connected us in our pain. And we know that we all need to be washed and receive a new vision of God.

When Jesus spoke this promise, I wonder if he also had in mind the first chapter of the Bible. Like his baptism, Genesis 1 describes all reality coming forth out of primal waters as the Presence of God hovers over the world like a dove.

And all that God makes, God sees as *very good*—as beloved and delightful. At creation's climax, God designs each person in

God's own image and *blesses* humanity. Every human is made as a glimpse of God, a blessed fractal of the divine face.

Is Jesus suggesting that if we've allowed our heart to be washed in these primal waters, God starts showing up everywhere we look in ever person we see?

This is what Mother Teresa discovered as she lost any sense of superiority and chose to keep loving others in the darkness. She wrote, "a clean heart can see God in each person. If we see God in others, naturally, we will love one another as God loves each one of us."

Similarly, the Hindu poet Balkrishna Sama, known as Nepal's Shakespeare, wrote, "I see God with my eyes wide open in the dear sight of every person."[8]

Jesus is suggesting just this. Once we stop striving to be on top and looking down on others, we're blessed to look upon the divine image in all humanity. The mundane and mystical merge into one. The sacred and secular, heaven and earth, return to their primal *union*.

Jesus promises that this divine vision is available to all who come clean. As we fall backward into the river of *metanoia* with other poor people, our eyes are opened to see God (Matthew 25:31-46).[9]

Breathed into God's Body

I stumbled upon Jesus' promise while wandering the way-stations of his path. It happened at the tail-end of one of the

---

8   Mother Teresa, *Where There Is Love, There Is God*, ed. Brian Kolodiejchuk (New York, NY: Doubleday, 2010), 16. I'm grateful to my friend Nikhil Mandalaparthy for sharing the Sama quote with me.

9   The Beatitudes are Jesus' first teaching in the Gospel of Matthew. Jesus' words in Matthew 25:31-46 are his final teaching. Together, they serve as the entry and exit of Jesus' Beatitudinal Way, the viewfinder of his spiritual vision. Notice that Jesus begins his movement by blessing the poor. He ends it by calling us to love the hungry, the thirsty, the unclothed, the foreigner, the sick, and the imprisoned. There is such a profound coherence to Jesus' Beatitudinal Way that often goes unnoticed. Overlooking it leaves our religion spiritually blind.

darkest nights of my soul: 2023.

This book began with my letter about how 2023 felt like a year-long winter in my life—dark, cold, and apparently dead. As imperfectly as I practiced it, compassion had stretched me wide open. Like Sade sang, I felt like "the king of sorrow, crying everyone's tears."[10] As I grieved and ached in the dark, I feared that I had been cut to the heart one too many times. The screwdriver was churning into me. My soul was vandalized. All good seemed gone.

That November, I was all-but-unwillingly on my way to the BitterSweet Retreat where I presented the first draft of this unexpected book. As I sat with my friend David on his porch late into the night, I told him that all I could see was the darkness. He listened patiently as I searched for words to describe the fear, pain, and confusion swirling inside me.

It was a mix of many things. The suffering of Ethiopia's civil war was overwhelming. In addition to the death and destruction, I knew that it was sending countless innocent children like Precious into the streets. A fresh wave of character assassinations and death threats had crashed over Lily's and my life again. I scrubbed my online platforms of family photos hoping to prevent them from being targeted.

Simultaneously, an acute fear of being abandoned by people I love was festering inside me. I was plagued with self-doubt and couldn't make progress on my next book. Identity theft, financial precarity, and my own sense of post-Covid mental muddiness haunted me. Then I learned that padre had cancer.

Lily's disappointment with exile was becoming darker and more severe. I so desperately wanted to make her *happy*. But I couldn't.

In my own soul, I went through my days with a chronic sense of emptiness. I'd find myself driving down the road

───────────

10 Sade, "King of Sorrow" track 3 on *Lovers Rock* (Epic, 2000).

contemplating how easy it would be to veer into the oncoming traffic and end it all.

Now on the porch in the darkness, I told David that I felt like my life was falling apart. I confessed, "I can't see where our path is headed."

I had turned forty earlier that year. On my birthday, David rebaptized me in Maine's cold waters, and I recommitted my life to following the Beatitudinal Way. But despite it all, I expected my life to be more "established" and "secure"—perhaps even "more blessed"—by this point. I felt like a failed adult in exilic America.

Our route was divergent. And all I had to show for this milestone in my journey was an enlarged compassion and negative certitudes laid bare by my life's erosion:

I don't know more than anyone else.

I'm not better than anyone else.

I'm just as poor as everyone else.

When I paused, David asked me, "What do you need?"

His compassionate question was unlocking for me. I immediately knew the answer. But I listed a few other things that made more sense and felt more respectable in my head: predictability, energy, togetherness.

Still, in my heart, I knew what I needed. I needed to *cry*. I needed my heart to flow and be cleansed with tears in the presence of my friend. *Grief must be witnessed to be healed.*

But I was too ashamed to admit this, to do this. Even with such a trusted friend. Even after he'd witnessed my grief so many times before. Even after he rebaptized me.

David then pivoted and invited me to do a brief breathing exercise with him. We inhaled deeply from our bellies. Then we exhaled freely from our chests. Slowly, in and out.

At last, we simply sat together in the silent darkness and waited on God.

I began to tremble in my seat.

Then to cry.

A river of electric energy surged through my body. It flowed out of my fingers like light.

As this calmed, I was transported in my consciousness. I saw a vision of God.

I beheld myself as a lung in God's chest. I watched as this quivering organ that I had become breathed in God's body. Inhaling and exhaling. Filling and emptying with pure divine oxygen.

I was fully at home in God. Completely connected and encompassed. Woven into the body of my Creator. I experienced the most solid embodiment and weightless levitation. All contradictions reunited into one. Pure union.

All of my fear melted away. I wasn't afraid of Lily dying. I wasn't afraid of my dad dying. I wasn't afraid of my own dear life falling apart. I wasn't afraid of all the horrific evil exploding in the Ethiopian civil war.

My past, present, and future reintegrated. I could remember my past but wasn't stuck in it. I could see into my future but wasn't ambitious for it. In this presence, I was at perfect peace. God was breathing me into total belonging.

And I could *see* it happening.

Then as my consciousness returned to the chair on the porch, I felt soft feathers gently brush across my face. The dove from Jesus' vision visited me.

My eyes filled with light in the darkness. I saw the sun rising over the treacherous mountains I had hiked the year before when, post-Covid, I couldn't breathe and my physical vision went blurry. A voice said to me, "Stay on the path."

This was the most intimate, blissful vision of God that I have ever seen. It was precisely what I needed in that prolonged, despairing chapter of blindness. Looking back, I can't help but notice when it appeared.

I had just confessed to my friend that I wasn't *better* than anyone else. That I didn't know *more* than anyone else. And that I was just as *poor* as everyone else.

This connected back to the moment when David rebaptized me in the Atlantic Ocean on my fortieth birthday. At that time, my inner life felt like Precious' old house: a small shack in an impoverished slum. Any sense of superiority to others had been washed away.

In that dark night of my soul, David guided me into a glimpse of Jesus' promise: when our heart is cleansed, God can show up. We can *see God*.

The purification process might feel blinding, like a baptism in darkness or being gouged in the eyes with a screwdriver. But what eventually manifests isn't a ruinous force radiating death. Heaven opens with a winged Presence of peace that expels fear, ends violence, and enfuses us with humane happiness.

It's as if we become a lung breathing in God's body.

Fully enfleshed.

Weightlessly levitating.

Electrified by a black-magic bliss weaving throughout the sadness.

A sacred shattering of the soul.

Isn't this the ecstatic end of our journey?

Crisis 6: Religion or Peacemaking?

Seeing God would seem like the climax of Jesus' Beatitudinal Way.

When his students caught a glimpse of his mystical vision, they wanted to camp out there and build a shrine around their experience. After all, what could be more blessed, more important and ultimate, than what the mystics came to call "the beatific vision"—the blessing of seeing God?

Isn't *this* the mountaintop of happiness?

In *The Essential Writings of Christian Mysticism*, Bernard McGinn collects over 500 pages of Christian mystical meditations from across the centuries and continents. A striking pattern quickly emerges.

Around 150 years after Jesus preached the Beatitudinal Way, the mystics began prizing the vision of God as the highest goal of the spiritual life. Their pursuit of this vision often eclipsed the importance of human relationships. It also fueled resentment of earthly life. An acute self-loathing and ugly punishment of the body appear across the tradition.

In a surprisingly short period of time, Christian mysticism became increasingly intellectual, elite, and otherworldly. We hear influential monks like Evagrius Ponticus (345-399) saying, "The kingdom of heaven is knowledge of the Holy Trinity co-extensive with the capacity of the intelligence."[11]

Don't worry if you can't understand what that means. It's a far cry from Jesus' opening annunciation that the kingdom of heaven is *good news for the poor*.

The repeated metaphor of the mystics is height: climbing above the human condition to leave this lowly world behind. Even

---

11 See Bernard McGinn, *The Essential Writings of Christian Mysticism* (New York, NY: Modern Library, 2006), 56.

so, mysticism could be militarized and justify atrocious violence.

Bernard of Clairvaux (1090-1153) was one of the most influential figures in medieval mysticism. And yet, sadly, he also co-founded the Knights Templar, an extremely powerful Christian military order. With his preaching, Bernard passionately promoted the violence of the Second Crusade.

As we've seen, Jesus was immensely mystical. He beheld *God* and said that we can too. But his mysticism points us in a refreshingly divergent direction yet again. His Beatitudinal Way doesn't stop with seeing God and soaring off somewhere else or justifying the unjustifiable.

For Jesus, a clarified perception of God reprioritizes *human* relationships and invests the struggle for *justice* in our world with even *more* value. After all, heaven opened while his flesh was immersed in a river with other people who were saying yes to John's way of justice.

Moreover, Jesus saw God *descending to earth* on his *body* as the dove of peace. This vision of heaven embracing his own beloved flesh propelled Jesus to return from the wilderness and start a public movement whose manifesto is the Beatitudinal Way.

Here we arrive at our sixth moment of decision, our sixth crisis, on our journey of becoming humanely happy: Will our faith fixate on spiritual experiences and dogmatic doctrines? Or will seeing our divine Parent inspire us to make peace as our life's work?

Said differently, will we look for God alone with our eyes raised above as we camp out in our religion? Or will we learn to see God in the faces of our enemy-siblings across the hostile boundaries we build here below?

This is the heart of Jesus' seventh and second-to-last blessing.

CHAPTER 9

Way-Station 7: Peacemaking

For Lily: Thank you
for teaching me to cherish peace.

"I would like us to do something unprecedented:
to create ourselves without finding it
necessary to create an enemy."[1]
James Baldwin

---

1 James Baldwin, *The Cross of Redemption: Uncollected Writings*, ed. Randall Kenan (New York, NY: Vintage Books, 2010), 251.

The Peacemaker's Path

Peace must be *made*. Peace never just "happens."

And Jesus isn't interested in religion that assumes it does. Peace is *work*. It's almost always extremely daring, daunting work.

Jesus signals this with his seventh blessing. In many ways, the previous six way-stations map how we *become* people who can actually *do* this daring, daunting work. Looking back on Jesus' Beatitudinal Way, we can see this with cleansed vision.

Peacemakers are afflicted with poverty just like everyone else. We aren't immune to suffering or exempt from emptiness. But we embrace the work of accepting that we're accepted by God. This doesn't start when we're on top. It starts when we have nothing left with which to elevate ourselves over anyone else. In our poverty, we slowly begin receiving the promise that the kingdom of heaven calls us poor people beloved and invites us into a new future of full belonging. Rather than being hardened by our pain and striving for appearances of invulnerability, peacemakers embrace being softened and opened to others.

Peacemakers step through and grieve our griefs. We process our devastating disappointments and express them with emotional honesty. We enter the haunted house of our trauma and receive the promise that we will be comforted, that an Advocate will accompany us and cry with us. With this promise, we resist allowing the powerful energy of our pain to boil into rage and break out with vengeance. Grief is the great unionizer of humanity and connects us with others. It slowly converts us into gentleness.

Peacemakers practice nonviolence with regulated power. We interrupt the imitation game and resist overcoming poverty and grief by impoverishing and grieving others. Our agency grows responsive and creative rather than reactive and combative. We begin trusting the promise that the whole earth will become our home. Slowly, we learn to accept that we don't need to dominate and displace others to feel safe. Nonviolence is our planetary future.

Still, peacemakers hunger and thirst for justice, here and now. We don't withdraw into passivity and resign the world to evil. We ache for right relationships of mutual flourishing. We dare to reimagine human identity, economic inequity, and political power. We immerse ourselves in this movement of *metanoia*. But as we crave for change, we learn to face our fear and trust the promise that we'll be fully satisfied in the end. We won't starve. And so, we resist becoming judgmental. We refuse to painish and condemn as we long for things to be right, even when they're not yet—and won't fully be until the end.

With this trust, peacemakers' ache for justice expands into compassion. Our heart opens to the suffering of others, whoever they are, and we choose to be a merciful presence in pain. We look inward with honesty at our own rotten capacity to do harm. We look outward with empathy at the suffering of others and the traumas they transmit in the harm they do. And we desire healing and repair for all of us. Despite everything, we belong to God. In the end, a mirror of compassion is promised to the compassionate, a balm for all wounds.

And through the dark nights of our souls—maybe the dark years or dark decades or dark lifetimes—peacemakers allow ourselves to be cleansed of all the residual superiority that clings to the pain of our poverty. This purifying process can feel blinding, like being buried in darkness and death. But Jesus promise us that the cleanhearted will see God. Nihilism is not the end. Humility opens heaven, and God will appear—not as a ruinous force but as the dove of peace who wings away all violence. Our divine Parent declares that we are beloved children, and we begin to see God in everyone. With time, we return from the wilderness with peace as our life's work.

In short, the Beatitudinal Way of Jesus makes us into people who can *make peace*. The peace of God becomes hereditary to our humanity—not merely an idea in our heads or a feeling in our hearts. Peace is no longer an ideology we passively endorse or an isolated activity we do among others. Peace is our Parent. Peace is our primal culture. Peace is our birthright. Our mandate. Our embodied ancestral craft.

When heaven truly opens, we realize that the divine dove is the presence where reality begins and returns. As we practice this presence, relationships of love and justice get woven throughout our poverty and tears, our vulnerability and longing, our anguish and ecstasy. We *become* these God-begotten humans in whom there is no violence—the unmistakable divine family resemblance.

The beauty and agony of the Beatitudinal Way reveals itself as the swelling womb of God. Peacemakers emerge from the labor as the baptismal water breaks. Like our brother Jesus, we newborn humans are moved to make peace our life's work.

We are God's beloved children.

Jesus' Seventh Blessing

Jesus' Beatitudinal Way is nearly home. Here he speaks his seventh blessing for his God-seeing listeners and all of us to hear: *Blessed are the peacemakers, because they will be called children of God.*

As we've seen, the first chapter of the Bible tells the primal story of God creating the world in seven "days." In many cultures, seven is the number of completeness. In the Genesis story, the seventh day comes after God creates all humanity in God's holy image. It represents a wholeness and peace that overflows with goodness.

Here God declares blessing over the entire cosmos. It's a moment of rest before the eighth day of creation begins: our human vocation to care for God's world.

I wonder if Jesus announced his seventh blessing as an echo of this seven-day creation story. Through this lens, we perceive that fullness isn't found in seeing God alone. After all, God is the other-embracing Creator of humanity and the whole universe. Fullness is found in becoming people of peace who can see *God's image* reflected in *every other person*. This is how we begin our primal vocation to care for the earth.

From this perspective, it makes perfect sense that Jesus promises that *these* people will be called *children of God*. People who labor for peace are God's offspring, the closest and clearest manifestation of divine DNA on earth.

These children are learning to glimpse God in every face, to see a sibling in every stranger—to recognize family in the foreign and fragmented. Peace has become our familial craft, the creative expression of what is born inside.

Jesus promises us that we will never be orphaned in this way of becoming human.[2]

Jesus' vision of God in the river mothered his message and movement of peace. He returned from the wilderness, introduced the Beatitudinal Way, and then expounded his vision of God as humanity's universally loving Parent. Divergent, Jesus taught:

> "You have heard that it was said, 'Love your countrymen and hate your enemy.' But I tell you, love your enemies and pray for those who persecute you, *so that you may be children of your Father in heaven*. God causes the sun to rise on the evil and the good, and sends rain on the just and the unjust." (Matthew 5:43-45)

---

2 It's worth noting that Jesus also seems to be alluding to a nationalistic promise to Israel about being "God's children" (Hosea 1:10). But instead of naming any ethnic, religious, or political group, Jesus says that peacemakers will be called God's children.

Behind this powerful statement, Jesus likely had in mind Moses' potent promise to Israel: "God will be an enemy to your enemies." This was the theological basis of Moses' religious nationalism.

After escaping Egypt, Moses claimed that the sun only shined on Israel when God destroyed their Egyptian enemies in total darkness. Then, on the brink of invading Canaan, Moses promised Israel exceptional rainfall to fuel their superior wealth as "more blessed" and "always at the top" of the nations. Finally, Moses told his people to "purify" themselves and activate this blessing by committing genocide against their Canaanite enemies.

This religious nationalism spawned King David's violent spirituality:

> "If only you, God, would slay the evil! Do I not hate those who hate you, Lord? I have nothing but hatred for them. I count them my enemies!" (Psalm 139:19-22; see Exodus 10:21-23; 23:22; Deuteronomy 28:12-13.)

This, no doubt, is what many in Jesus' original audience expected and *wanted* to hear him say. But after seeing God for himself, Jesus was emboldened to dramatically revise Moses' nationalist vision of God.

When our hearts are truly purified, we see the God of heaven who gives sunshine and rain to *all*—whether they deserve it or not, whether they're "good" or "evil." The God of heaven doesn't promise to be an enemy to our enemies. Our "enemies" are actually *siblings* in *our* Parent's family. And so, God commands us to love "them" *as ourselves*.

Notice that God commands this because of *who* God *is*. *God's* behavior is determined by God's character—not by the character of others. God isn't a reactive force that conforms to external patterns and pressures like a billiard ball. God is the

Creator of the universe who parents all humanity with love.

And this is precisely what Jesus declares God's unchanging character to be: *God is kind to the ungrateful and wicked* (Luke 6:35). This is the clearest definition of divinity that Jesus ever gave. Those who don't bother to acknowledge God's gifts or actively ruin them are still met with our Parent's kindness. This is *who* God is and so *how* God behaves.

For Jesus, the most essential elements of life—from light to water—are incarnations of this radical divine love that suffuses and sustains our world. If this is *who* God is, then this is *how* God's *children* reveal themselves: they love their enemy-siblings. They ask our Parent for the wellbeing of *everyone* and *work* for it, even for those who seek to harm them.

This love is the genetics, psychology, and politics of divinity. This is the character of peace on earth.[3]

With Jesus, we discover that seeing God for ourselves is a conversion experience. Once the vision sinks in, violence is no longer part of the picture. The othering of religious nationalism is noxious to our divine DNA and vanishes.

In short, we *become* people of peace who can make peace as our family practice with all others as our sacred siblings.

Jesus' Practice of Peace

This vision of God birthed and raised Jesus' own practice of peacemaking.

If we survey the three years of his public movement, it's difficult to single out a specific "program" of peace, because peacemaking pervades it all. Jesus never gave a formula or

---

3 Visit iffglobal.org/love-your-enemy to explore three resources that may be helpful for our practice of enemy-love: (1) "Self-Awareness Inventory," (2) "35 Practices of Enemy-Love," and (3) "Enemy-Love Reading List." I extensively discuss Jesus' vision of enemy-love in my book *Reviving the Golden Rule: How the Ancient Ethic of Neighbor-Love Can Heal the World* (Downers Grove, IL: IVP Academic, forthcoming).

"strategic plan" for peacemaking, as valuable as these resources may be. He taught the Beatitudinal Way and lived his life. *There it is.*

And perhaps *that's* the point: on Jesus' Beatitudinal Way peacemaking isn't merely an ideology we endorse or a set of tactics we employ. It's our way of becoming who we are. It's as universal and particular as our evolving humanity.

Its core is that primal divine creativity that calls us beloved.

So, how did Jesus make peace in his society?

It's clear that Jesus' peacemaking began with himself. Having survived acute trauma, there was no other way. He went out to the wilderness, wrestled with his demons, and got baptized by John. There he discovered who God really is and who he really was.

Once his identity as God's beloved child was secure and his public movement began, Jesus continued prayerfully cultivating his inner life. He took time to rest and to grieve his suffering. He avoided unnecessary conflict and kept himself safe until his time came. As Etty Hillesum said, he "reclaimed large areas of peace"[4] in himself before anything else.

Fresh from the wilderness, Jesus hand-picked a cohort of student practitioners.

Divergent, Jesus recruited the most polarized people in his society: zealous religious nationalists, an imperial collaborator, blue-collar workers, a cynic, a doubter, a mystic, a betrayer, and others on the spectrum of humanity, including many women. These people became the first pilot of his peacemaking movement.

We see that, having done his own inner peace work, Jesus wasn't intimidated to bring these polarized people together. They lived, ate, worked, and traveled together as a family. Jesus taught them, "Be at peace with each other" (Mark 9:50). After starting

---

4 Hillesum, 218.

with his own soul, Jesus' peacemaking moved into intimate relationship, the place where it's often most difficult and most transformative for us to practice.

The daily spiritual practice that Jesus taught his students, what we call the Lord's Prayer, was an exercise in peacemaking, both within the self and between our selves. It began by invoking our universal belovedness and belonging in God: "*Our* Father in heaven..." It ended by renouncing the addictions that drive us to conflict: "kingdom, power, and glory." Its center was self-awareness and depolarizing compassion: "forgive us as we forgive others."

In this prayer, there are no "others." Mindfully practicing it washes away any sense of superiority and enmity. It recenters us in our collective core identity: we are we, beloved children of *our* Parent. This was Jesus' most elemental invitation to the art of peacemaking.[5]

The habits of Jesus' daily life were also practices of peacemaking:

> He attended scandalous dinner parties where othered people were welcomed and valued as insiders.
>
> He traveled outside the boundaries of the "holy" land and shared compassion with the indigenous people Moses marked for genocide.
>
> He helped reintegrate people whose mental illnesses and society's stigmas had estranged from community.
>
> He spoke forgiveness to people who made him suffer and seemingly deserved to be damned.
>
> He valued broken bodies, fed hungry bellies, and relieved

---

5   I unpack Jesus' brilliant spiritual practice in my book *Flourishing on the Edge of Faith: Seven Practices for a New We* (Washington, D.C.: BitterSweet Collective, 2022).

physical suffering—whether it was religiously acceptable to do so or not.

Jesus wept with the grieving and spoke hope to the heartbroken.

As we've seen, Jesus' peacemaking ached for justice and confronted injustice. Like the prophet Jeremiah, he refused to say "peace, peace" where there was no peace. He publicly critiqued the predatory politics of the ruling establishment and unmasked the greedy, heaven-closing hypocrisy of the religious elite. Like John, he taught the redistribution of wealth to meet basic human needs. Abundance is for equity not accumulation: this is the banking system of heaven.

Jesus also disrupted the structural violence in the temple that closed space for the poor. He confronted the cultural violence of his society by telling stories that honored the othered. He protested direct violence by defending women from men's murderous "purity" laws and weeping over Jerusalem when it chose conflict over peace.[6]

From start to finish, Jesus resisted surrendering to violence and turning God into another weapon of human power. He rebuked his still-nationalistic students for wanting to use physical force to punish their ethno-religious opponents. When his students still didn't get it and tried to kill to protect him from arrest, Jesus shouted, "No more violence!" (Luke 22:51). After his arrest, he confronted his oppressors with uncowered presence and pointed questions. Still, Jesus refused to conform and copy their way.

In the end, Jesus' death endures as his ultimate act of peacemaking. It's really the nucleus of every node on the

---

6 For the seminal analysis of cultural, structural, and direct violence, see Johan Galtung, "Cultural Violence," *Journal of Peace Research*, Vol. 27, No. 3 (August, 1990), 291-305.

Beatitudinal Way—his poverty, his grief, his nonviolence, his justice, his compassion, his cleanhearted solidarity with sinners, his vision of God.

We watch as Jesus gets arrested, condemned, tortured, and executed before a jeering crowd. For Christians, it's a scene of heinous wickedness, a repugnant crime cutting to the core of reality: people kill God's beloved Child.

What could be more deserving of violent prevention or punishing retribution than *this*?

But Jesus converts this murderous atrocity into the ultimate demonstration of God's unconditional love. On the cross, Jesus shows that God is who Jesus saw God to be: kind to the ungrateful and wicked. This is heaven's way of unkillable life.

In case we missed it, we see this ultimate truth once and for all: *God is not a killer.* God isn't an "enemy to our enemies." God doesn't "break out" against "the evil." God doesn't mimic and mirror human condemnation, painishment, and death.

God is *our* Parent in whom there is no violence.

And so, God descends in this bloody crime scene as the dove of peace. God isn't the cosmic Victimizer. God is the innocent Victim who has every right to damn God's enemies to hell but cries out for their peace in heaven. As Whitehead saw, "God is the great companion—the fellow-sufferer who understands."[7]

As the culmination of his own practice of the Beatitudinal Way, then, Christ's cross ends the repetitive imitation game of violence and re-opens humanity to God's creative love forever. In this way, the death of Jesus—his apparent *defeat*—becomes the paradoxical triumph of his peacemaking in which none are humiliated.

Jesus proved in the most intimate, ultimate way possible

---

7 Whitehead, *Process and Reality*, 351.

with his own body that humans can do their very worst. And still, God isn't violent and doesn't save with violence. God's salvation is the presence of love, even in pain, free of vengeance.

A balm for all wounds.

Paul of Tarsus, himself a former religious nationalist who presided over the execution of people othered with the belittling label "Christian," would call this "the gospel of peace." After his own mystical vision, Paul saw Jesus' death as a cosmic act of "peacemaking" that embraces everything in the entire universe. Thereafter, Paul started preaching "the *God* of *peace*" across the boundaries of the Empire (Romans 15:33; Colossians 1:19-20; 2 Corinthians 13:11; 1 Thessalonians 5:15; Ephesians 6:15).

And so, from the very beginning of his movement, Jesus promises us that peacemakers will be *called children of God*. We may intensely fear being labeled as radicals and rejected as traitors. The way of the peacemaker is no joke. But no othering, no violence, no death can orphan or alienate us. Peacemakers incarnate an irrevocable, cellular covenant with God that reveals who God really is and who we really are.

These imperfect people have learned to see God not only in prayer with their eyes closed. They see God even through pain in the faces of their enemy-siblings. And so, like Jesus, they refuse to condemn and conform to conflict. They devote their agency—their creative craft—to seeking healed relationships, restoring justice, and *making peace*.

If you want to see what God looks like, observe how peacemakers live and die. *Theirs* is the divine DNA—an unweaponizable, anti-supremacist lineage of becoming humanely happy. They are blessed with an unbreakable belonging in God and a cosmic security that isn't vulnerable to any human identity theft.

Crisis 7: Approval or Persecution?

Here on the "seventh day" of Jesus' path of new creation, peacemakers may receive his seventh, seemingly summative blessing. But there's an "eighth day of creation"—a new beginning that calls us deeper into our care for creation.

And here peacemakers face our seventh and most excruciating moment of decision. Our seventh crisis. It's the most radical rub.

Peacemakers are rarely popular or met with approval. Moses' way of blessing was sacrosanct in his society and seemingly still is in ours today. What's the outcome of this old but ever-novel beaten path?

Jesus was murdered. So were most of his first practitioners. So were many of our most memorable peacemakers: Mahatma Gandhi, Etty Hillesum, Dietrich Bonhoeffer, Medgar Evers, Martin Luther King Jr., Óscar Romero—just to name a few.

In Pakistan, the fifteen-year-old Malala Yousafzai was shot in the face by the Taliban. She narrowly survived this horrific assassination attempt.

Alexei Navalny, a follower of Jesus who dared to expose high-level corruption in Russia, was jailed and killed in one of Putin's prisons. Navalny said that he wanted to "turn up the volume of heartbreak to the maximum." And so he did—with his own dear *life*—by refusing to surrender to injustice.

This is a disturbing but unmistakable pattern.

We might expect people who make peace to be celebrated or accepted or at *least* politely brushed aside. But the reality is often the opposite.

This is especially so in systems that promise prosperity and pump religious nationalism as the path to peace: *peacemakers are routinely held in suspicion and marked as dangerous.* Many are denounced, ironically, as "anti-peace." After three short years of peacemaking, Jesus was condemned by the guardians of Zion for "subverting the nation" (Luke 23:2).

Why is this?

As we've seen from the start, it seems that we're addicted to the beaten path. We're addled by the "blessing" that prosperity-driven religious nationalism promises us. Deep in our bones, we *desire* to be "more blessed" than "others." We *want* to be "on top." We *long* for "God" to be "the enemy of our enemies."

As James Baldwin saw with serrated insight, "Men have an enormous need to debase other men." Or as he said differently, "When the prisoner is free, the jailer faces the void of himself."[8]

Of course, we devoutly deny this truth and piously insist on the opposite. We're offended by the suggestion that we worship a "tribal God" or want to degrade "others" to avoid facing the emptiness in ourselves. Maybe *they* do. But not us!

Still, if only in our subconscious bone marrow, we often crave superior status and supreme strength, *not* the equal belovedness of God's children. The lure of religious nationalism and the promise of prosperity arouse some of our deepest drives and suppressed insecurities.

I suspect our addiction to othering is rooted in our unprocessed poverty. This is the place where Jesus' Beatitudinal Way unpleasantly but brilliantly begins. If we bypass this trailhead, we remain trapped in our desperate, if only half-conscious, awareness of being small, vulnerable, mortal creatures. We feel like maybe if we could just make it to the top, we would finally feel safe. There and then, we could finally forget that we're dying, just like everyone else.

And so, when a "peacemaker" comes along who interrupts

8 Baldwin, *Collected Essays*, 392, 563.

our addiction, we might be intrigued and even inspired for a spell. Jesus' audience was. But if they're truly serious and call us to surrender these dependencies for the sober way of divine love, we often find the withdrawals intolerable.

In fact, like us addicts typically do, we may feel existentially *threatened* and directly *attacked*. "Peacemakers" become *enemies*. We quickly label them with all sorts of nasty names in pursuit of our inhumane happiness.

And so, we react with all the righteous fury we can muster. We insist that "God" is on our side. And with this weapon of mass destruction in our arsenal, we claim the mandate to eliminate these damned heretics, traitors, and "anti-peace" terrorists. As one politician recently wrote on Israel's American-supplied rockets, "Finish them."

The prosperity gospel and religious nationalism coagulate. God and genocide gel.

Before traveling onward to our final way-station, Gandhi, King, and Romero offer us an instructive case study of this repetitive pattern.

These were three very different people: a Protestant preacher, a Catholic priest, and a Hindu lawyer. They struggled for peace in three very different places: against British imperialism in India, against racial segregation in America, and against military dictatorship in El Salvador. But all three men sought to become humanely happy in Jesus' Beatitudinal Way. Gandhi said that he studied Jesus' words every day of his adult life.

And all three got assassinated for much the same reason: their *peacemaking* directly challenged the *supremacist identities* and *militarized power* in their societies. The negative "peace" of injustice insisted that we'd be safer and happier without them.

As Baldwin wrote with piercing clarity, "the future is like heaven—everyone exalts it but no one wants to go there now...

it has always seemed easier to murder than to change." We relentlessly resist "doing something unprecedented: to create ourselves without finding it necessary to create an enemy."[9]

We like our saints dead.

However ominously, then, this takes us to our seventh and final moment of decision on Jesus' Beatitudinal Way, our climactic crisis: Will we surrender peacemaking to preserve our society's approval in the status quo? Or will we risk becoming unrecognized and opposed by our own communities as the price of just peace?

Said differently, will we idolize an earthly identity? Or will we allow God's DNA to change our lives and transform us into citizens of the kingdom of heaven?

This is the heart of Jesus' eighth and ultimate blessing.

---

9 Baldwin, *Collected Essays*, 251, 698.

CHAPTER 10

Way-Station 8: Persecution

For the victims of Ethiopia's civil war.
See you soon.

"Two roads diverged in a wood, and I—
I took the one less traveled by,
And that has made all the difference."[1]
Robert Frost

---

[1] Robert Frost, "The Road Not Taken" available online at https://www.poetryfoundation.org/
poems/44272/the-road-not-taken.

Becoming the Enemy

I glimpsed where Jesus' Beatitudinal Way goes in the nightmare of Ethiopia's hellish civil war.

Before the war broke out, othering was escalating to fever pitch. Not far from us, a man was lynched in public and strung up from a traffic light. In another nearby city, a woman poured kerosene on a man's brutalized body and burned him alive in a public square.

At the time, I was working as a professor of public theology and ethics at the flagship graduate school of theological education in Addis. But as the crisis intensified, I knew that I couldn't stay safe on this evangelical island.

I resigned in 2018. After the grueling grief work that I did in 2019, Lily and I and our friend Tekalign Nega started the Neighbor-Love Movement. NLM advocates for love, justice, and flourishing for all Ethiopians—regardless of differences in ethnic, religious, and political identity.

Our message was and remains simple: the other person is not our enemy; the other is our *neighbor*. We invite our audiences to sign our Neighbor-Love Covenant and to commit themselves to embody this way of love in everyday life. This work begins with seven practices rooted in how we see, hear, and speak with others.[2]

We traversed Ethiopia and shared this invitation wherever doors would open. It all started in a city hall not far from Somalia. From that unexpected point of origin, we went to public universities, Bible colleges, faith centers, a business incubator, government institutions, libraries, civil society organizations, and a feminist collective. We engaged with influential activists, powerful politicians, senior religious clerics, ordinary individuals, and entire families.

---

2 To learn more about the Neighbor-Love Movement, our Covenant, and Practices, visit www.nlmglobal.org.

Soon, NLM took off in ways we never imagined.

Thousands of Ethiopian youth signed the Neighbor-Love Covenant and committed to being Neighbor-Love Ambassadors. (This is our term for everyday peacemakers.) Our social media campaign reached over twenty million people online. We won a small grant from the European Institute of Peace, and the Ethiopian government's Orwellian Ministry of Peace started talking with us about expanding our work. We began producing a show about neighbor-love for one of Ethiopia's most popular TV channels.

The response to our message was overwhelmingly positive. In the face of Ethiopia's crisis of othering, we were extremely encouraged. It felt like a dream of peacemaking was being born in a crucial turning point in Ethiopian society. Neighbor-love seemed to be becoming a *movement*.

I'll never forget Ethiopia's Attorney General, Gedion Timothewos, signing our Covenant and telling me, "Andrew, this work is as timely and important as it gets." Ethiopia's Chief Commissioner of Human Rights, Daniel Bekele, echoed him: "This could not be more important. You should go with full force." As conflict escalated, NLM published our "Joint Declaration for Human Value and Nonviolence in Ethiopia," and over a hundred Ethiopian leaders signed their names to it.

Maybe *peace* could be *made*, after all?

But this all changed quite literally overnight once the grief boiled over and the war exploded. Many of our Declaration's signers started loudly championing the war in the name of "saving" Ethiopia. Most simply went silent. One of our closest partners asked us to write a formal letter declaring that she had nothing to do with us.

Officials who once encouraged our message brazenly

defended atrocities and war crimes as "peace" and "justice." The Ethiopian government issued an Emergency Decree declaring that giving "moral support to the enemy" was a criminal offense. Of course, calling for peaceful negotiation with "the enemy"—rather than violently exterminating them—could easily be construed as "moral support." People were understandably afraid, and I don't judge them.

Our calls stopped being answered. Texts were no longer returned. Doors closed. We never heard from the TV channel about our show again. *Poof.*

What I experienced personally pales in comparison with what millions of Ethiopians suffered and are still suffering as I write these words with Selam in my heart. But it was a mindbending, heartbreaking experience nevertheless. It nearly took me under and helped me to appreciate Jesus' final blessing with a new sobriety.

Powerful Christian leaders and media influencers with hundreds of thousands of followers started spreading false stories about me. They said that I was a CIA agent. Or working for the Egyptian government. Or being paid millions of dollars by insurrectionists. The details of the story varied wildly. But the plot was always the same: I was a dangerous threat with a "hidden agenda" to overthrow the Ethiopian government.

A "documentary" about me soon appeared on YouTube. It rapidly started spreading across social media platforms. It showed pictures of me and narrated an ominous script about my "mission to destroy Ethiopia." The video quickly racked up over 50,000 views.

More painfully, professional colleagues and people I considered personal friends accused me of supporting terrorists. A smiling theologian, who had signed the Neighbor-Love Covenant, published an article claiming that I find "pleasure" in

Ethiopians' suffering. Another said that I had deceived Ethiopia about who I really was.

We had spent *years* working together, and I thought we trusted each other. But that trust evaporated in seconds.

My office mate, who previously greeted me with hugs in the hallway and shared lunches with me at the cafeteria, wrote that I should be detained and deported. Senior religious leaders—again, people who had signed NLM's Covenant and our Joint Declaration—insisted that I was a liar with malicious intent toward Ethiopia. The former director of the graduate school where I had taught demanded that I make a public apology to all Ethiopians for the "harm" I had caused them. In his message, he emphasized that I had specifically "harmed" *Christian* Ethiopians by opposing the war.

Then a viral media personality—believed to be employed by the Prime Minister himself—made a series of shows about me. My friends in the security sector tell me this was payback for my article in *Foreign Policy* critiquing the Prime Minister's Christian nationalism.[3] He strung together absurd lies in his attempt to "prove" that I was behind a high-level political assassination and massive religious schism rocking Ethiopian society. (For example, he said I'm a citizen of Norway, a country I've never visited, and linked me to Norwegian people whom I've sadly never met.) The absurdity would have been hilarious if the situation weren't so serious.

Throughout these years, I received over fifty pages of death threats. Most came from fellow Christians who insisted that their belief in "God" and the "peace" of their country *required* them to kill me. A radioactive blend of the prosperity gospel and religious nationalism had literally been militarized. It fueled the twenty-first century's deadliest conflict in which 1.2 million people died—

---

3 Andrew DeCort, "Christian Nationalism Is Tearing Ethiopia Apart," *Foreign Policy*, June 18, 2022.

1.5 times the number of victims in Rwanda's infamous genocide.

The war online was a crucial battlefront for the war on the ground. Character-assassinating videos functioned like drone strikes. Viral media campaigns worked like ambushes. Private messages and public articles operated like psychological snipers.

This wasn't unique to me. Anyone who advocated for peace was accused of being banda (a traitor) and attacked as an agent of "the enemy." The famous Ethiopian singer Dishta Gina—one of the few who used his platform to appeal for peace—was pressured to appear on TV and tearfully apologize for his transgression. Ironically, it was the same TV channel that had ghosted NLM once the war broke out.

After my name appeared on a government blacklist amidst ongoing death threats, Lily and I, Tekalign, and our board decided that it was time for us to transition out of Ethiopia. My peace advocacy would need to continue in American exile now.

These were disorienting, soul-concussing years. As I wrote in my opening letter to you, it felt like I was being repeatedly stabbed in the heart with a screwdriver. After three decade-like years of this soul vandalism, I was plagued with self-doubt, insecurity, and the fear of being abandoned by people I love.

I had been told countless times that I was evil, demonic, and hellbent on destroying others. I was publicly branded as the antithesis of a peacemaking child of God.

And these attacks were finally hacking their way into my heart. It was an identity theft far more devastating than anything that happened to our bank account. I learned that gaslighting, being repeatedly told that you're someone you're not, is an extremely powerful weapon of war.

It became more and more difficult for me to do things that once came so naturally: to sleep, to speak, to write, to meet with other people. I battled with a powerful impulse to withdraw and hide.

More painful, my work had cost Lily her home and access to her family. The disappointment I saw etched in her face day after day is difficult to describe. I feared that both of us were withering away. Maybe finished forever.

In the process of beginning to write this book, I found myself wrestling with maddening questions:

> *Was the Neighbor-Love Movement a massive mistake?*
> *Should I have never raised my voice for peace and justice in Ethiopia?*
> *Am I done now—too impoverished inside to be of any good to anyone anymore?*

The title of my previous book—*Flourishing on the Edge of Faith*—felt like it was mocking me. I floundered in practicing what I preached. I was not flourishing.

Jesus' Eighth Blessing

In this strange place of character assassination, socio-political displacement, and apparent hopelessness, Jesus speaks one last blessing. It's perhaps his most divergent. It returns to the first, and the Beatitudinal Way ends where it begins. As Herman Hesse wrote, "In all beginnings a magic is hidden."

To the poor who have become peacemakers, Jesus declares, *Blessed are the persecuted for the sake of justice, because theirs is the kingdom of heaven.*

The ending of Jesus' Beatitudinal Way is brilliant but fearsome. It isn't health, wealth, and winning, at least not in the usual senses of these happy words. It's not ascending to the top and everyone else wishing they were you. It isn't pride, prosperity, and power.

The final way-station on the path is standing out for justice and being *persecuted* for it. The word Jesus uses here literally means to be targeted and chased away.

What a queer trajectory Jesus charts for becoming humanely *happy*! It moves from cringing in poverty to being chased away by persecutors!

We see at last that when we walk the Beatitudinal Way to the end, we are deconformed to the prevailing patterns of popular culture. We become different kinds of people. This path changes us.

At a certain point, we'll likely be labeled and lose our tribe. Our life may become unrecognizable and offensive to the dominant loyalties that define our society. Our deepening commitment to peace and justice, including with "the enemy," may get us into serious trouble. We become *banda* or *persona non grata*—the disgraced, disinherited, unwanted "others."

We look back and discover that the seven decisions on Jesus' Beatitudinal Way are highly consequential. We may not realize this at first. But they alter who we're becoming.

The trajectory of our lives gets rerouted in these critical moments of pathmaking. As these choices compound, we find ourselves traveling a different path altogether. We may even walk apart from family, friends, and fellow believers with whom we assumed we shared the same road.

Jesus' Beatitudinal Way decisively diverges from our tribal religion, culture, and nation.

This is the only blessing that Jesus himself comments upon. He offers a thumbnail sketch of how persecution plays out. It remains as predictable today as it was in first century Palestine:

> "You're blessed when people insult you, persecute you, and falsely say all kinds of evil against you because of me.

Rejoice and be happy, because great is your reward in
heaven! For in the same way, they persecuted the prophets
who were before you." (Matthew 5:11-12)

Persecution begins with insults. These are the "harmless"
pokes, jokes, and labels we use to mark others as *other* or not-
quite-*us*.

Then misinformation and false stories start circulating.
Before you know it, full-blown disinformation and conspiracies
swirl about who you *really* are, what you *really* want, and what
you're *really* trying to make happen. It's character assassination—
psychological, social, and political identity theft.

At some point, death threats may start. You become a
target, and people take action. They chase you away or try to kill
you. In fact, they likely feel a sense of moral *obligation*—perhaps
even *religious* or *Christian* obligation—to end you.

If we see persecution with compassion, this is what their
(*our*) supremacist worldview requires of them (*us*). We're all
addicts to othering.

What Do You Truly Love?

Here at the end of his way, Jesus is describing a fundamental
clash of values. It's a conflict over the outcomes of this fiery path
of choices that he's led us down. These choices add up to what we
believe is worthy of our ultimate love and loyalty.

And here's the rub again.

The confusing thing is that people at war often use the very
same words to talk about what they claim to love: "God," "peace,"
"justice." But we use these loaded words with very different
meanings. In fact, the clash is precisely about the very meaning
of peace and justice. Really, it's all a clash about who *God* is and
what *happiness* truly means.

Is the heart of peace and justice *really* the restoration of right relationships for our mutual flourishing? And is this because *God* is actually *our* Parent who descends as a dove when all superiority is washed away? And so, is *happiness* truly found when we hear our Parent call us all beloved children and learn to love even our enemy-siblings as our divine DNA?

Or, are peace and justice *really* about being in control over others and punishing those who oppose us? And is this because "God" is a selectively benevolent, violent force that favors us as the enemy of *our* "enemies"? And so, is "happiness" truly found in pride, prosperity, and power?

Jesus has the integrity and compassion to be honest with us: the Beatitudinal Way will deconform and transform us. It will unmake and remake us. We may no longer fit into familiar places that once felt like home. Our people might stop recognizing us. We might find ourselves insulted, character-assassinated, and chased away.

We might not even recognize *ourselves* in the aftermath.

Once again, this blessed rage for (dis)order usually comes back to those critical moments of decision on Jesus' path for becoming humanely happy. They're the places between the logs where the fire burns hottest:

1. What did we do with the pain of our poverty? Did it harden us? Or did it open us to the vulnerable, volatile emotions within us?

2. How did we process our grief, if we did? Did it boil into vengeance? Or did it soften us into nonviolence?

3. Let's say it did the latter. When the ache went deep, did

we withdraw into passivity? Or did we hunger and thirst for justice?

4. Where did our craving for justice lead? Did it strain toward condemnation? Or did it stretch out with compassion?

5. When all we could see was darkness, what then? Did we crumble to cynicism? Or did we plunge into humility and open our eyes to see God like never before?

6. Let's say we catch a glimpse of God. Do we camp out in our religion and build a shrine around our purified identity? Or do we welcome the divine DNA of peace to flow through our veins and fuel our life's work?

7. These six questions all culminate in the seventh crisis: When peacemaking isn't rewarded or even *wanted*, what is our true love after all? Said differently, what is our *Love* that defines all of our other loves—our *Happiness*? Is it approval, belonging, supremacy—what Jesus called "kingdom, power, and glory"? Or have we actually begun internalizing that the poor are precious to the God of heaven? And so, have we learned to entrust our vulnerable lives to this God? That is, have we accepted that we have nothing to lose and nothing to prove and that our true love and only enduring happiness is found in God and others and the way of just peace? Even with our enemy-siblings? And even when it costs us *everything*?

Those first exits are extremely enticing to us humans: hardening, raging, withdrawing, revenging, resigning, religioning, warring. The religious exit may be especially tempting for readers of this book.

But when we take any of these exits, we'll feel existentially threatened by Jesus' way of humane happiness. Divergent, his path will strike us as going backwards or racing off the map and over the cliff into the abyss.

There is little we humans fear more than this process of *metanoia*. It demands being unmade and remade by the Happiness of heaven's love that only truly appears when all superiority to anyone else is gone.

As Baldwin wrote, "Any real change implies the breakup of the world as one has always known it, the loss of all that gave one an identity, the end of safety."[4]

Here in this place of utmost vulnerability, Jesus dares to bless those who are persecuted for justice. He promises us that we will be perfectly safe and finally at home in heaven's kingdom.

In fact, he calls out to us, "Rejoice and be *happy!*"

Choosing delight is our defiant protest. We saw it in Alexei Navalny, who joked, smiled, and formed his hands into a heart in the face of one of the world's most brutal tyrants.

Persecuted humanity has now become *prophetic*, just like the peacemakers who came before us. We unveil reality and reveal what is truly precious. Even if we're mislabeled, even if we're lied about, even if we're chased away, even if we're reduced to the ultimate poverty—death itself—that primal peace of our divine belovedness opens to us and will embrace us all without end.

Despite everything, we belong to God. The prophets of justice are invincible. Its martyrs, in body or soul, are immortal. As Etty said in the face of Auschwitz:

"Essentially, no one can do me any harm at all. Yes, children,

---

4 Baldwin, *Collected Essays*, 209.

that's how it is. I am in a strange state of mournful contentment."[5]

Ours is the kingdom of heaven.

The End Is Hidden in the Beginning

This clash over the meaning of ultimate happiness begins playing out from the start of Jesus' movement.

We watch as he preaches an inspiring sermon in his hometown church. He names God's liberating love for the poor, oppressed, and brokenhearted. It sounds like the beginning of the Beatitudinal Way.

Jesus' audience hung on his words. Their hopes were rising. They thought that Jesus might be their Messiah. Could this be the new Moses?

But Jesus continued his sermon and confronted his audience's religious nationalism. That is, he challenged their claim to an exceptional identity and special favor with God. He dared to say that God loves foreigners and enemies just as much as God loves them. In fact, Jesus said that, if forced to choose, God would prioritize the *others* that the blessed insiders had excluded. If you don't believe me, you can read the story in Luke 4:14-30.

The reaction was predictable. It matches the pattern we often see today. Jesus' hometown audience was so outraged that they dragged him out of town and tried to throw him off a cliff. They literally wanted to trash Jesus.

When this didn't work, they started spreading rumors about who Jesus *really* was—a foreigner himself? Insane? Demon-possessed?

Death threats and assassination attempts quickly followed. The rest is history.

---

5 Hillesum, 288.

As I've indicated repeatedly in this book, Jesus was a revisionary teacher. He *re-saw* things to their divergent roots.

And so, he taught a revisionary *identity*. According to Jesus, we're all equally beloved. And we all need to undergo a transformative process that begins in our poverty.

And Jesus taught this identity based on his revisionary *theology*. The God of heaven creates, loves, and blesses *all* of us, including the ungrateful and wicked. The sunshine and rainfall incarnate this divine Reality.

This theology leads to a revisionary way of becoming *human*. It's poverty-processing, tear-soaked, nonviolent, hungry-and-thirsty, compassionate, God-seeing peace and justice. Humane happiness isn't winning. It's learning how to relate to one another as if we're all actually beloved and the Beatitudinal Way is actually *blessed*.

Jesus' community found these divergent revisions to be blasphemous betrayals. They called it "subverting the nation" and worthy of death (Luke 23:2).

It seems most of us do. We're addicted to our religious nationalism, prosperity gospel, and the othering they desperately depend upon. We'd rather follow the beaten path, not Frost's "road less traveled." And that, too, makes "all the difference."

Again, the bottom of our disorder is our unprocessed *poverty*.[6] It's our entirely natural, divinely designed need to feel secure in our *personal worth*. But we so easily shoot this up by seeing others as unrelated or less than ourselves. It's the cheapest and easiest trip to a sense of significance. T.S. Eliot saw this with rare clarity:

"Half the harm that is done in this world is due to people

---

6   T. S. Eliot, "The Cocktail Party" (1948), Act 1, Scene 1.

who want to feel important. They don't mean to do harm; but the harm does not interest them. Or they do not see it, or they justify it because they are absorbed in the endless struggle to think well of themselves."[7]

We want to be *more* blessed. To stand on *top* of the hierarchy. To use *force* when our "blessing" is threatened. Even to claim that our enemy-making "*God*" set it up this way, damn it all. This othering ideology makes us feel important in our endless struggle to think well of ourselves.

Whoever questions our "holy order" (the literal meaning of *hierarchy*) we tend to label as foreign. Unfaithful. Revisionist. Heretical. Radical. Unjust. Anti-peace. Even terrorist. Recall Gandhi, King, and Romero.

Meanwhile, our "justice" murders the messiah and sometimes unleashes genocide in the name of "God."

I believe this is why Jesus begins his divergent Beatitudinal Way by *blessing* us in our poverty. This is our universal human condition.

And perhaps only the *pain* of our poverty—when faced with the promise that we're unconditionally loved by our Parent precisely when we have nothing to elevate us over anyone else—is powerful enough to deprogram the othering mindset, to knock us off the beaten path.

This blessing reorients us into a new way of becoming humanely happy. This happiness doesn't depend on being better than others. Its prosperity doesn't need to be "more blessed" than anyone else. It opens us toward a shared grief. Then a gentle nonviolence. Then a restorative justice. Then an expanding

---

7 I'm grateful to Dan Snyder for the phrase "the bottom of our disorder." See his beautiful book *Praying in the Dark: Spirituality, Nonviolence, and the Emerging World* (Eugene, OR: Cascade Books, 2022).

compassion. Then a healing vision of God. And then a practice of just peace that can survive othering's persecution.

When we accept that we're actually wanted by God, even when we have nothing but our cringing selves, then we have truly nothing to prove, even if everyone else is wanted too. We also have nothing to lose, even if we lose seemingly everything else for the sake of this Beatitudinal Way. Worth is compounding rather than competitive in the kingdom of heaven.

And so, this way of becoming humanely happy doesn't give up, even when it leads to *us* becoming the *other*. We see now that this is precisely where Jesus' path ends up.

But through his seven way-stations, we've entered into a more beloved identity and secure belonging than othering, religious nationalism, the prosperity gospel, and their violence can fathom or touch. It's that strange state of mournful contentment that's ultimately invincible to persecution.

Even when you're labeled and lied about, you're identified and known by God. Even when you're attacked and insecure, you're held safe with God. Even when you're chased away and suffering seems final, you're wanted by God. Even if you lose your people, your belonging, your home and sense of self, heaven knows who you are and will welcome you home forever. In a nutshell, *blessed are the others*.

Coming Home

Jesus brilliantly ends his Beatitudinal Way where he begins it. He speaks the same blessing to the persecuted that he spoke to the poor: *yours is the kingdom of heaven*.

But now, our poverty is chosen rather than merely suffered. We have accepted the suffering, because we've chosen to renounce the beaten path that produces it: othering, supremacy, and violence.

The poor and persecuted face the same primal fear: that

we're unwanted and ultimately destined for permanent precarity and pain. That may appear to be our lot in this first round of our human journey here on planet Earth. It often does, to me at least.

But earthly appearances can be deceiving. To the poor, the persecuted, and everyone in-between, Jesus promises, "*Yours* is kingdom of heaven."

The Beatitudinal Way offers us the clearest compression of what Jesus understood the kingdom of heaven to be. It's our unconditional belovedness and belonging with our Creator, one another, and everything in all creation.

This happiness is what Jesus believed lives forever. It's the unkillable manifesto that he declared from the very beginning of his revolutionary movement:

1. The poor are beloved.
2. The grieving are comforted.
3. The nonviolent belong.
4. The justice-hungry are fed.
5. The compassionate are mirrored with compassion.
6. The cleanhearted see God everywhere in everyone.
7. The peacemakers are called God's children.
8. And the persecuted come home to everlasting happiness.

This is what lives in the kingdom of heaven. This humane happiness is what Jesus promises us.

But Jesus is kind enough to be honest: persecution is a likely detour if we're willing to travel toward the kingdom of heaven.

We're not looking for it. We don't want it. But the Beatitudinal Way deconforms us. It might appear to deconstruct and destroy us. It irritates othering, upsets prosperity, and enrages religious nationalism.

As so often, James Baldwin probed to the heart of the matter:

"It is precisely at the point that when you begin to develop a conscience, you must find yourself at war with your society. It is your responsibility to change society if you think of yourself as an educated person... The war of an artist with his society is a lover's war, and he does, at his best, what lovers do, which is to reveal the beloved to himself, and with that revelation, make freedom real."[8]

The fiery path of Jesus makes freedom real. Having revealed to us from the beginning that we are God's beloved, he finally calls out to us, *Rejoice and be happy!*

Don't be afraid. God delights in all of us poor people. Doom is not our destiny. Happiness is eternal.

And so, Jesus goes all the way to a violent execution on the cross. He subverts our nation with his gospel of peace. And he invites us to follow.

Here at the end of the Beatitudinal Way, we discover that death is nothing to fear. It's like walking through a door or changing clothes or flipping a light switch. Death is so gentle, so trustworthy, so merciful when we're held by heaven. Death is but a gateway to the God of peace who loves the poor. When our eyes open, birth and death are the same thing. YOLF! *You only live forever.*

From this perspective, it's never okay to kill, but it's always okay to die. From beginning to end, from poverty to persecution, from cringing inside to being chased away—the promise of heaven has been spoken.

This is the way of becoming human. This is our truest happiness. This is our fullest flourishing, our most authentic wellbeing, our best life—now and always.

This is the heart of *everything*.

---

8 Baldwin, *Collected Essays*, 685, 672.

CHAPTER 11

Onward: The Beatitudinal Way

For Katie and Evangeline: Thank you
for showing me the erosion can be beautiful.

"Go back to where you started, or as far back as you can.
Examine all of it, travel your road again and tell the truth
about it. Sing or shout or testify or keep it to yourself:
but know whence you came."[1]
James Baldwin

---

1 Baldwin, *Collected Essays*, 841.

The Beatitudinal Way is Jesus' invitation to become humanely happy. It's how our humanity wants to burn in the mysterious fire of life. This is his call to come home to a fierce flourishing that never finally dies.

But the Beatitudinal Way is divergent to almost everything we've been taught about the blessing of happiness, even by our most authoritative teachers. No wonder Jesus warned that his path would be unpopular and often left untraveled (Matthew 7:13-14).

Still, there's sacred perception, power, and promise in this eightfold path. Jesus invites us to enter in to it and to let it enter into us. His invitation is to trust it to the end in the face of our deepest fears. To let it change us rather than conforming it to our painishing path of being human as we've known it.

And how powerful the pull to the beaten path is:

> to escape the vulnerability of our poverty
> to become hard and suppress our suffering
> to find safety in violence
> to corrupt justice
> to criminalize compassion
> to collapse into cynicism
> to make something less than peace our life's work
> to idolize the approval of others as the empty
> end of our journey.

It can be a slow drift or a dramatic departure.

From this perspective, Jesus is making an ultimate claim on our humanity. But he's also making a very radical promise to us. He's assuring us that the people who choose to live divergent to this dead-end are actually *blessed*. They will be eternally *happy*.

Of course, this path will be misunderstood, discredited, and sometimes brutally attacked. Even by family, friends, and fellow believers. There's no longer any surprise in this fearsome fact.

But Jesus isn't afraid. And he calls us to face our fears.

With the courage he gives us through his promises, we can choose to live this way. In our invisible inner worlds. In the webs of our interpersonal relationships and work. In our local cultures and global systems. In our ultimate hopes for where our planet is moving and what our humanity can become.

To the people who do, Jesus declares, *You are the salt of the earth... You are the light of the world* (Matthew 5:13-14). These prophetic people preserve our humanity and turn the lights on in reality.

For now, we might look like unhappy fools and unlucky losers. I certainly did in 2023.

But earthly appearances can be deceiving. Like the prophets before us, we can practice what's truly precious in life and point our fragile family forward to our cosmic destiny. We can become what W.H. Auden called "paradigms now of what a plausible Future might be."[2]

As James Baldwin surveyed Jesus' Beatitudinal Way, he wrote, "The revolution which was begun two thousand years ago by a disreputable Hebrew criminal may now have to be begun again by people equally disreputable and equally improbable."[3]

That can be us.

That can be now.

For all of us.

Everywhere.

Always.

We can begin the revolution again.

---

2 W. H. Auden, "The Garrison," in *Epistle to a Godson, and Other Poems* (New York: Random House, 1972), 24.

3 James Baldwin, "The Fire Next Time" in *James Baldwin: Collected Essays*, ed. Toni Morrison (New York, New York: The Library of America, 1998), 312.

This is the way.

***

Dear _____ (kindly insert your name once more),

As I write this, it's 2024, and I feel like I've completed a cycle on the Beatitudinal Way. Here at the harvest, I'm back at the beginning, learning to do my "first works over" as Baldwin admonished.

My dad recently died, and I've rediscovered my poverty. In this painful process, I'm finding out afresh what I truly love and actually believe about becoming happy. I'm "traveling my road again and telling the truth about it."

Do I need to be more than an "other" to be okay with myself?

Will I become hardened by the pain or grieve again?

Is nonviolence still my choice, or will my sadness boil into enraged vengeance?

Only time can tell. But I'm committed to the practice. I've never wept or laughed more freely. I feel like Andrew again, like God's beloved child, liberated from the fear of what once was. Shameless.

Based on its brilliant design, I discern that Jesus' Beatitudinal Way is *meant* to be practiced *cyclically*. The end returns to the beginning: the kingdom of heaven. There's simply too much here to be fully integrated in one go of it.

And so, like all primal practice, we need to work through it, over and over again, until this path becomes who we are, our second nature and truest, transitional self. Creative repetition is the essence of transformative practice.

I suspect we may need to work through the entire Beatitudinal Way several times before our earthly journey ends.

And we may find ourselves in different places at different times. All of Jesus' eight way-stations are intimately interconnected, and we can transition between each of them in a nonlinear trajectory.

Two thousand years into his young movement, there's so much more here to discover.

I offer this book to you in hopes that we can discover it together.

For now, I return to my own practice in the springtime of a new year. The winter has broken. I feel again that dearest freshness after being haunted by my deepest fears. The agony of a long labor is turning into the joy of new birth. I can hear the music once more. The river is flowing.

I'm in a strange state of mournful contentment.

Let us walk together, whoever we are, wherever we find ourselves, in this endlessly transitional journey of becoming humanely happy. Whatever happens, I'm learning to trust Bonhoeffer's blessed witness from his Nazi prison cell: *Despite everything, we belong to God.*

We are not alone. We are not insane. We are human.

Ours is the kingdom of heaven.

Blessings!
Andrew

APPENDIX 1

Beatifying Everyday Life

For Obi, Dave, Avery, and Greg: Thank you
for making the work beautiful and functional.

"Ultimately, we become what we pay attention to...
Practice tends to make permanent."[1]
Curt Thompson

---

1 Curt Thompson, *The Soul of Shame: Retelling the Stories We Believe about Ourselves* (Downers Grove, IL: IVP Books, 2015), 48.

People across cultures use "Blessings" as a salutation, both online and in person. This word expresses a beautiful kindheartedness. But often enough, "blessing" can feel like a superficial well-wish with little deeper meaning.

What if we practiced using the word "blessing" with more intentionality? Rather than a generic sign-off, cheap consumer product, or trite religiosity, each time we use *blessing* can serve as a mnemonic device in our everyday lives to help us remember Jesus' invitation to walk the Beatitudinal Way. This little word can be refilled with the humane happiness that Jesus promises us.

I hope that after reading this book, "Blessings" is imbued with fresh meaning for you. Each time we use or encounter it, let's allow this word to reroute us into Jesus' divergent path.

Blessings!

APPENDIX 2

Charting the Beatitudinal Way

*For the Herkinds-Heaths: Thank you
for hearing the symphony over the car bombs.*

"I do believe that everyone
Has one chance to f*ck up their lives.
But like a cut-down tree, I will rise again
And I'll be bigger and stronger than ever before."
Jonah and the Whale[2]

2 Jonah and the Whale, "The First Days of Spring," track 1 on *The First Days of Spring* (Vertigo, 2009).

This chart offers an overview of the interconnected dimensions of Jesus' Beatitudinal Way. In a sense, Jesus' eightfold path moves downward to the right and then back up to the left. As we end, we begin again. We emerge from our initial being into a new becoming.

The Beatitudinal Way is an endlessly expanding spiral galaxy of transformation until we're fully home and truly alive in heaven's everlasting happiness.

	Us Humans	Our Fears	Jesus' Promises	Our Choices
1	The poor	Being othered with permanent pain and precarity	Theirs is the kingdom of heaven	Become hardened or grieve?
2	The grieving	Being overwhelmed and unwanted in our pain	They will be comforted	Become vengeful or nonviolent?
3	The nonviolent	Being dominated and displaced	They will inherit the earth	Become withdrawn or hungry and thirsty for justice?
4	The hungry and thirsty for justice	Being disappointed and imitating injustice	They will be filled	Become condemning or compassionate?
5	The compassionate	Being unmirrored and alone in our misery	They will be mirrored with compassion	Become cynical or cleanhearted?
6	The cleanhearted	Being blinded to God and goodness	They will see God	Become religious or make peace?
7	The peacemakers	Being misidentified and rejected as anti-peace	They will be called children of God	Become approved or persecuted for justice?
8	The persecuted for the sake of justice	Being othered with permanent pain and precarity	Theirs is the kingdom of heaven	Become hardened and hopeless or happy and prophetic?

APPENDIX 3

Reading Scripture for Every Good Work

For Peter: Thank you
for helping me hear the music.

"The life-choices and situations embedded in the [biblical] text are not ignored or neutralized... but serve as pivots for moral reflection. Teaching is thus more than the transmission of information or even the deepening of the students' humanity. It may also bestow an example of freedom and responsibility."
Michael Fishbane[1]

---

1 Michael Fishbane, *The Garments of Torah: Essays in Biblical Hermeneutics* (Bloomington, IA: Indiana University Press, 1989), 120.

My Christian theology works with a critical commitment to the Bible as inspired Scripture. I realize this approach may be unfamiliar to some readers. This appendix briefly unpacks my simplest understanding of what the Bible is and how to read it. My approach is profoundly indebted to Michael Fishbane, my wizard-like professor of Hebrew Bible at the University of Chicago.

The Bible describes at least three things as being "God-breathed" or *inspired*: the first humans (Genesis 2:7), Jesus' first disciples (John 20:22), and the Bible itself (2 Timothy 3:16).

What does this mean?

The first humans were God-breathed. God created them from the dust and gave them God's own conscious life.

But this divine inspiration didn't override their God-given freedom to alienate themselves from God, one another, and how to be humanely happy. They quickly did (Genesis 3), and this alienation climaxed in murderous violence: Cain killing his brother Abel (Genesis 4).

Likewise, Jesus' disciple Peter was God-breathed. Jesus' act of breathing God's Spirit into his students was meant to represent the new creation of humanity. Peter was among them and honored as their leader.

But this divine inspiration—direct from Jesus himself!—didn't prevent Peter from remaining entrenched in religious nationalism and racial prejudice, even after Jesus' death and resurrection. (See Matthew 16:21-23, Matthew 26:50-54, and Acts 10, especially verses 34-38.) Peter's errors were so severe that Paul felt compelled to publicly critique the God-breathed Peter to Peter's face and in his own God-breathed writings (see Galatians 2:11-16).

The Bible itself, then, clearly shows that being "God-breathed" doesn't mean being "perfect" or invulnerable to deviating from God's desire. It means being given as a beloved gift of God and being invited into cooperation with God's own Spirit *but always with our God-given freedom to reject God's way.*

If this is so, then we shouldn't be surprised that our God-breathed Bible includes teachings—for example, killing children and committing genocide—that clearly don't reflect the character of God embodied in Jesus and revealed in Jesus' Torah. Like Paul to Peter, Jesus directly confronted many of these problems in Scripture immediately after introducing his Beatitudinal Way. He declared, "You have heard that it was said [in Scripture and tradition]... But I say to you..." (Matthew 5:21-48).

No wonder Jesus was driven out of town, threatened with death, and ultimately crucified (see Luke 4:14-30). What was his religious leaders' charge against him? "Subverting our nation" (Luke 23:1-2).

In this way, we can see that Paul was being very precise when he wrote, "All Scripture is God-breathed and is useful for teaching, rebuking, correcting and training in justice, so that the servant of God may be thoroughly equipped for every good work" (2 Timothy 3:16).

Paul says that God-breathed Scripture is "useful" *not* "perfect." And its usefulness is to train us in *justice*, so we can be equipped for *every good work*. The point is more about ethics than ideology.

How do we know what "justice" and "good work" look like? They are clearly summarized in Jesus' Beatitudinal Way, his larger Sermon on the Mount, and his entire life, teaching, death, and resurrection revealed in the Gospels.

I would add that part of the Bible's brilliance in including seriously problematic content is that reading it forces us to wrestle with these crucial questions: "Who is God? What is justice? How do we serve God and do good work?" As Professor Fishbane wrote, "The life-choices and situations embedded in the [biblical] text are not ignored or neutralized... but serve as pivots for moral reflection" that claim our "freedom and responsibility."

In other words, God-breathed Scripture provides a challenging mirror in which we can look our God-breathed selves directly in the face and confront this painful but profoundly important reality with our God-given freedom: "Look how we put words in the mouth of God and justify injustice that doesn't reflect God's good work."

In this way, Scripture is even more *useful* than it would be if it were "perfect" and didn't include the disturbing, disorienting content that it actually does.

I hope this brief essay clarifies that I love the Bible, that I respect the Bible, and that I take the Bible extremely seriously as God's inspired gift for us. This is why I've spent many years of my life learning Hebrew, Greek, and how to interpret the Bible.

Part of what it means to be genuinely *biblical* is to *critique* the Bible, which the Bible itself brilliantly does. Like the Beatitudinal Way, the Bible is more complex and challenging than we often imagine. Both deserve better of us.

That's what I'm inviting us to do with this book and my work. I hope you'll continue traveling with me, even if you don't agree with everything that I write.

Questions for Reflection

*For Anne: Thank you
for seeing my soul at the Bellfry. Glory!*

The following questions are designed to help you reflect on what you've read, discuss it with others, and begin integrating Jesus' Beatitudinal Way into the evolving version of who you're becoming. Don't feel like you need to cover every question; engage with what stirs something in you. Thanks for sharing your time and attention!

A Letter From Me to You

1. Andrew described 2023 as the hardest year of his life. His soul felt vandalized by fear, pain, and doubt. Have you ever experienced a season like this in your life?

2. How have these seasons affected you? What did they do to the person you're becoming?

3. Late in 2023, Andrew discovered that he was in a long labor that was birthing something totally unexpected in him: this book. Is something being birthed in you through your painful experiences of human labor?

The Trailhead to the Way

1. Blessing can be described as authentic happiness, full flourishing, the good life, true wellbeing, fulfilled humanity. How would you describe blessing in your own words?

2. How do you react to "Jesus"? Do you feel inspired, allergic, or something else?

3. What do you think of the four reasons Andrew gave to take Jesus and his Beatitudinal Way more seriously?

4. Jesus' eightfold path is brilliantly interconnected and invites us into a transformative process of becoming human. Have you ever seen Jesus' Beatitudes like this before? How might this orientation unlock his teaching in new ways for you?

5. Andrew highlighted seven existential choices or "crises" hovering between the blessings in Jesus' eightfold path.

Where do you feel most afraid or tempted to exit?

6. Jesus' Beatitudinal Way is divergent to the beaten path of othering, the prosperity gospel, and religious nationalism. How does this sit with you? How have these powerful forces affected and maybe even (con)formed or killed your faith?

Way-Station 1: Poverty

1. Do you ever think of yourself as "poor"?

2. Andrew took us into Precious' house and her family's experience of poverty. What forms does poverty take in your life? Consider making a list.

3. What is surfacing in you as you acknowledge and explore your poverty?

4. Where do you find yourself in your journey of accepting that God accepts and loves you? Can you trust that the kingdom of heaven is promised to you exactly as you are, including in all of your poverty? What doubts and fears are attacking your trust?

5. Crisis 1: Have any impoverishing experiences tempted you to harden yourself and seek to become invulnerable? How might they have softened and connected you with others in unexpected ways? How do you want to respond to the pain of your poverty?

Way-Station 2: Grief

1. Have you ever "stepped through" into your haunted house of grief? Describe your experience.

2. What did you discover inside yourself? Consider finding some silence and stillness to make a list of your griefs. Remember that grief is the great unionizer of humanity; Jesus wept. You are not alone.

3. How do you grieve as the unique person that you are?

Who do you allow to witness your grief?

4. Andrew described reremembering his grief-stricken experiences and visualizing God as an Advocate who was there beside him and crying with him. What might happen if you reremember your painful experiences like this? Consider giving it a try. If you want to go a step further, write a letter to God about your grief.

5. Crisis 2: Are there any griefs in your life that are trying to harden you, enrage you, and make you vengeful?

Way-Station 3: Nonviolence

1. How have you seen the imitation game of conflict play out in your own life or society?

2. Popular culture often represents nonviolence as weak, ineffective, and utopian. But Chenoweth discovered that nonviolence is twice as effective as violence in bringing sustainable change and always works when just 3.5 percent of a population practices nonviolence together. What comes to mind when you think of "nonviolence"? How might Chenoweth's research challenge popular perceptions of it?

3. Andrew defined nonviolence as power that's characterized by responsive creativity rather than reactive conformity in the face of conflict. How would you describe nonviolence in your own words?

4. Jesus rooted his teaching of enemy-loving nonviolence in God and God's character. How do you imagine God? Do you believe that God is completely nonviolent? Or does your God inflict violence on "enemies" to accomplish God's will?

5. Jesus gave five examples of how we can practice nonviolence: (1) assert confounding solidarity (walk the second mile), (2) stand your ground (turn the other

cheek), (3) rescript your language (bless those who curse you), (4) practice radical generosity (give your coat), and (5) depolarize how you see the "other" and yourself (forgive as you are forgiven). Which of these practices feels especially relevant for you? How do you want to practice nonviolence in your own life?

6. Etty Hillesum described how practicing nonviolence made her harmless and unharmable. How does her story inspire or challenge you to trust Jesus' promise that the nonviolent will inherit the earth?

7. Crisis 3: Nonviolence makes us vulnerable. What fears of being dominated or displaced surface in you when you consider committing to Jesus' practice of nonviolence? What forms might withdrawal or resignation be taking in your life?

Way-Station 4: Justice

1. Have you ever felt hungry and thirsty for justice like Selam's story illustrates? What's your story?

2. Andrew defined justice as right relationships of mutual flourishing. How did you understand justice before reading this chapter? How do you understand justice now?

3. What was most challenging or inspiring to you about Jesus and John's "way of justice"? Recall that John centralized human equality, economic equity, and responsible power.

4. Jesus promises us that the hungry and thirsty for justice will be fed. When have you experienced satisfaction in your craving for justice?

5. Crisis 4: Where do you observe judgmentalism or condemning others in your life? Have you ever found yourself trapped in the cycle of painishment? How might your craving for justice expand into a new compassion?

Way-Station 5: Compassion

1. Etty Hillesum and Dietrich Bonhoeffer experienced extraordinary suffering as they struggled for justice. And yet, their lives expanded into a more radical compassion. They refused to "other" the "others," examined their own "rottenness," and chose empathy even for their executioners. What inspired or challenged you in their stories?

2. Andrew described compassion as the willingness to be present with others in pain. How do you understand compassion?

3. Jesus practiced radical compassion with all the "wrong" people, including a Canaanite woman marked for genocide. Have you ever experienced this radical compassion? Who is your "Canaanite," and how do you want to practice compassion with them?

4. How do you understand Jesus' death? What is saving about this horrific event of violent injustice?

5. Crisis 5: Selam's story illustrates how blinding the practice of compassion can be when we're unmirrored. Do you ever feel tempted to shutdown and close your heart? What is your relationship with cynicism?

Way-Station 6: Cleanheartedness

1. Mother Teresa experienced acute anguish, spiritual doubt, and nihilistic despair in her journey of practicing compassion. Have you ever had a dark night of the soul? Describe your experience as honestly as you can.

2. "Purity" is a loaded term and easily reminds us of harmful "purity culture." How do you understand purity or cleanheartedness?

3. Andrew wrote that humbly abandoning the appearance of purity can be the surest proof of actually being pure. How does this help you reimagine purification or cleansing?

Have you ever had a "blinding" experience that stripped you of feeling superior to others but ultimately opened your eyes to a new vision of God?

4. Jesus saw God and promised that we can see God when our hearts are cleansed. Have you ever had a mystical "baptism" like Jesus when he heard God say, "You are my beloved child" and saw God appear as the dove of peace? What stood out to you in Andrew's experience of becoming a lung in God's body?

5. Crisis 6: Are you ever tempted to build a shrine to your spirituality and erect a wall around your religion? Is "seeing God" the mountaintop of faith, or is there something more? Where do you observe religion becoming self-serving instead of serving the God of peace?

Way-Station 7: Peacemaking

1. Each of the previous six way-stations on Jesus' path prepare us to become people who can *make* peace. Pause to review them: (1) reckoning with poverty, (2) processing grief, (3) practicing nonviolence, (4) struggling for justice, (5) expanding into compassion, and (6) cleansing the heart to see God. Which of these way-stations are especially important for you as you seek to become a peacemaker?

2. Andrew presented Jesus' entire life as an integrated practice of peacemaking. Which aspects of Jesus' peacemaking were especially inspiring or challenging to you?

3. Jesus promises that peacemakers will be called children of God. Have you ever felt misnamed or orphaned in your peacemaking? When have you experienced God's parental care in your peacemaking?

4. Peacemakers can grow into glimpsing God in every face and seeing a sibling in every stranger. Have you ever

experienced this? How might you actively refocus your eyes to see others with this divine vision?

5. How do you understand "the kingdom of heaven"? How might it be unconsciously tethered to othering, the prosperity gospel, and religious nationalism? How might it offer you radical hope in the face of these addictions?

6. "Love your enemy" was probably Jesus' most challenging teaching. Try to be extra honest: Who do you see as enemies? How might you actively commit to loving your enemy-siblings?

7. Crisis 7: What is your relationship with the approval of others? Are you willing to be disliked, excluded, or even persecuted as you seek just peace? What are you actively doing to cultivate the courage necessary to persevere as a peacemaker? Think creatively!

Way-Station 8: Persecution

1. Jesus' vision of being blessed or humanely happy is seemingly upside-down. It travels through poverty toward persecution. How does this make you feel? How might it inspire you to reimagine the blessing of authentic happiness?

2. Andrew wrote that when you love the enemy, you become the enemy. Have you ever experienced or observed this pattern? What stands out to you from Andrew's story of being persecuted for seeking peace and justice in Ethiopia?

3. T.S. Eliot wrote, "Half the harm that is done in this world is due to people who want to feel important." What is your relationship with feeling important? How might your natural desire for significance be fueling conflict within yourself and with others?

4. What do you truly love? What is your Love that defines all of your other loves?

5. How do you process Jesus' claim that people who are persecuted for seeking justice become prophetic and truly happy? Do you trust his promise that the kingdom of heaven belongs to these divergent people?

6. Andrew wrote that when we trust that we're held by heaven, death becomes like walking through a door, changing clothes, or flipping on a light switch. It's no longer something to fear. How do you feel about dying? How might you grow into a more loving relationship with "the last enemy"? Is it okay to die?

7. Crisis 8: What will you do with the pain of persecution and the poverty it brings? Are you willing to return to the beginning and rewalk Jesus' Beatitudinal Way?

Onward: The Beatitudinal Way

1. Jesus' Beatitudinal Way invites us to change. How has traveling his path with Andrew changed you? How has your imagination for true blessing and happiness evolved?

2. What remains tempting to you on the old beaten path of human culture? Take a moment to check-in afresh with the othering, prosperity gospel, and religious nationalism that may remain lodged in you.

3. What's the next step that you need to take on Jesus' Beatitudinal Way? Is there a way-station that you're being invited to "do over again" as Baldwin wrote? Your deep desires and lingering fears can be important (re) starting places.

Author Biography

Andrew DeCort has been called
a dissident theologian by his
friends. His work is deeply
inspired by Dietrich Bonhoeffer,
his writing by James Baldwin,
his spirituality by Etty Hillesum.

Andrew received his PhD in religious and political ethics from the
University of Chicago. In 2016, he founded the Institute for Faith
and Flourishing in Chicago. In 2019, he co-founded the Neighbor-
Love Movement in Ethiopia. IFF and NLM have reached over
twenty million people with the invitation to nonviolent spirituality.
Andrew has taught ethics, public theology, peace and conflict
studies, and Ethiopian studies at Wheaton College, the Ethiopian
Graduate School of Theology, and the University of Bonn.

Andrew is the author of *Reviving the Golden Rule: How the Ancient
Ethic of Neighbor-Love Can Heal the World* (IVP Academic,
forthcoming), *Flourishing on the Edge of Faith: Seven Practices
for a New We* (BitterSweet Collective), and *Bonhoeffer's New
Beginning: Ethics after Devastation* (Fortress Academic). His
words have appeared in *Foreign Policy, the Los Angeles Review
of Books, the BBC, The Atlantic, The Economist, Christianity
Today, Comment Magazine, Sojourners, The Other Journal,
Wheaton College Magazine, The Journal of Religion, Political
Theology, All Africa, BitterSweet Monthly,* and numerous other
platforms. Andrew writes the newsletter Stop & Think at andrew-
decort.com. He lives in Chicago with his wife Lily, a gentle spirit
and luminous painter.

www.ingramcontent.com/pod-product-compliance
Lightning Source LLC
Chambersburg PA
CBHW031516120626
46545CB00005B/1901